Passing the Tests of Life is a sound
walking with Christ. Despite man's
of adversity, this book attests to th
come numerous obstacles but also to ....
win. Each chapter offers an encouraging word that will boost the confidence of readers from all walks of life.

This book is undeniably intended for those seeking answers to many of life's questions, specifically those who feel as though they have reached a glass ceiling in their spiritual walk. Get ready to break the glass! Bishop George Davis hands over the tools for overcoming each test and standing against Satan's attack.

Leave the defeated attitude by the wayside! This book provides the key to unlocking the door of advancement, increase, and bountiful blessings by simply overcoming the simple trials of life. Bishop Davis explores ways to overcome each potential hindrance in order to grow closer to our heavenly Father, and he does so in a manner that is easy to follow and understand. This is definitely the book to read!

—JESSE DUPLANTIS
DESTREHAN, LA

Passing the Tests of Life is a vitally important book for all believers. Every Christian goes through the twelve tests that are introduced in this remarkable book, including The Disappointment Test, The Offense Test, and The Confrontation Test. Passing these tests will determine what level of success you do or don't have in your Christian walk. Not only should you read this book, but you should also encourage others to do the same.

—BISHOP KEITH A. BUTLER
SENIOR PASTOR OF FAITH4LIFE CHURCH, DALLAS AND AUSTIN, TX

Step-by-step, George Davis shows us how to conquer life's challenges and places us in the winner's seat—in the perfect will of God. This book is intended for anyone, without regard to his level of spiritual maturity, who seeks to gain promotion in the kingdom of God. *Passing the Tests of Life* not only dispels the idea that God is the author of man's struggles, but it also allows readers to acknowledge the blessings that can be birthed out of challenging situations. Easy to read and highly informative from beginning to end, this book will have its audience captivated until the final chapter. Look no further for the answers to spiritual increase because they are contained within these pages!

—MARILYN HICKEY
INTERNATIONAL EVANGELIST AND HOST OF *TODAY*
WITH MARILYN & SARAH

Passing the Tests of Life can definitely be labeled a guidebook intended for those seeking to go higher in the things of God. The truths revealed in this book propel readers out of a state of defeat and mediocrity into a life of total success, increase, and peace. This book is not for the Christian who is content in his or her current spiritual lifestyle, but for those thirsting for all God has in store for them. I have known George for many, many years, and he has a way of explaining "winning" principles in a way that causes people to be encouraged and inspired to go out and conquer the world. If you are looking for hope that you have not reached a plateau in life but that there is so much more for you, then read this book!

—MARK HANKINS
MARK HANKINS MINISTRIES, ALEXANDRIA, LA

No one likes feeling like they've hit a ceiling in their life, like things will never get any better than they are. If you're one of those people who are sitting around saying, "There must be more than this," please know that there is! My friend and brother George Davis will guide you step-by-step to the life you have always believed was possible in his new book, *Passing the Tests of Life*. Don't continue another day going around in circles. Let today be the first day to the best days of your life!

—ANDRÉ BUTLER
SENIOR PASTOR, WORD OF FAITH INTERNATIONAL CHRISTIAN CENTER
SOUTHFIELD, MI

I have served with George Davis in ministry over the last seventeen years, and I have always been impressed with his honest, heartfelt, and practical teaching style. You can see that he is living the Word that he preaches. With the release of *Passing the Tests of Life*, he has unlocked the mystery to that nagging question, Why do I keep going through this? This book should be on the bookshelf of every person who is tired of going through the same trials, obstacles, and hurts over and over again. It's a "how-to-win" book that provides simple yet profound truths to address life's most common, confusing, and complicated tests. Once you read this book, you'll be able to recognize the test and pass it with confidence and finality.

—JOEL GREGORY
SENIOR PASTOR, FAITH CHRISTIAN CENTER, SMYRNA, GA

As a former NFL player, I realized that the Bible is most important. It's my life, my food; without it I could quickly fall away. I have sat under the teaching of Bishop George Davis, and my life has been enriched with the wisdom he has deposited into my life. Like a playbook,

Passing the Tests of Life will show you the Xs and Os of life. It will teach you how and when to play offense and defense. Bishop Davis, like any coach, wants you to win, and his book will help you succeed in the game of life.

—MAURICE WILLIAMS
FORMER NFL OFFENSIVE TACKLE, JACKSONVILLE JAGUARS

There is more to playing in the National Football League than the game. I have a family, relationships, investments, and a future that could disappear with one unfortunate play or bad life decision. There is pressure to living a godly lifestyle. Why? Because millions of people are watching my moves, analyzing my decisions, and listening to my words. I am eternally grateful to Bishop George Davis for showing me how to look to the Word of God as my source. In his newest book, *Passing the Tests of Life*, he will equip and condition you with time-less truths that will put you in position to make winning plays on and off the field.

—RASHEAN MATHIS
NFL CORNERBACK FOR JACKSONVILLE JAGUARS

PASSING
the TESTS *of* LIFE

GEORGE DAVIS

CHARISMA
HOUSE

Most CHARISMA HOUSE BOOK GROUP products are available at special quantity discounts for bulk purchase for sales promotions, premiums, fund-raising, and educational needs. For details, write Charisma House Book Group, 600 Rinehart Road, Lake Mary, Florida 32746, or telephone (407) 333-0600.

PASSING THE TESTS OF LIFE by George L. Davis
Published by Charisma House
Charisma Media/Charisma House Book Group
600 Rinehart Road
Lake Mary, Florida 32746
www.charismahouse.com

Unless otherwise noted, all Scripture quotations are from the King James Version of the Bible.

Scripture quotations marked AMP are from the Amplified Bible. Old Testament copyright © 1965, 1987 by the Zondervan Corporation. The Amplified New Testament copyright © 1954, 1958, 1987 by the Lockman Foundation. Used by permission.

Scripture quotations marked NIV are from the Holy Bible, New International Version. Copyright © 1973, 1978, 1984, International Bible Society. Used by permission.

Scripture quotations marked NKJV are from the New King James Version of the Bible. Copyright © 1979, 1980, 1982 by Thomas Nelson, Inc., publishers. Used by permission.

Scripture quotations marked NLT are from the Holy Bible, New Living Translation, copyright © 1996, 2004, 2007. Used by permission of Tyndale House Publishers, Inc., Wheaton, IL 60189. All rights reserved.

Scripture quotations marked THE MESSAGE are from *The Message: The Bible in Contemporary English*, copyright © 1993, 1994, 1995, 1996, 2000, 2001, 2002. Used by permission of NavPress Publishing Group.

Cover design by Justin Evans
Design Director: Bill Johnson

Visit the author's website at www.georgedavis.org.

Library of Congress Cataloging-in-Publication Data:

Davis, George (George L.)

  Passing the tests of life / George Davis. -- 1st ed.

      p. cm.

  Includes bibliographical references (p.   ).

  ISBN 978-1-61638-613-9 (trade paper) -- ISBN 978-1-61638-723-5 (e-book) 1. Providence and government of God--Christianity. 2. Opportunity. 3. Success--Religious aspects--Christianity. I. Title.

  BT135.D295 2012

  248.4--dc23

                                        2012006300

13 14 15 16 — 10 9 8 7 6 5 4

Printed in the United States of America

Dedication

THIS BOOK IS dedicated to the most precious gift in my life after Christ—my wife, April, and our three children, Keragan, Kaden, and Kasden. No one will ever truly know how much you sacrifice to allow me to serve the needs of so many others. Thank you for your tireless support and for making our home the "greatest getaway on Planet Earth."

My greatest joy is allowing God to use me to keep a smile on your faces. My prayer is that God will continually grant all the desires of your heart and make your every dream come true. No assignment or ministry opportunity will ever come before you. I love you for life!

Contents

Acknowledgments

THERE ARE SO many people who have added, and continue to add, significance to my life and inspire me to be God's best that I could never mention everyone by name. I sincerely thank my wife, April, for being my best friend in the world and the ultimate sounding board. You always find a way to make me believe even more in what God can accomplish through me.

Thank you to my mom, Sandra Wilbourn, and my dad, Perry Davis, for introducing me to Christ at Greater Mount Carmel Missionary Baptist Church in Detroit, Michigan. Thank you for teaching me to love all people at all times. Your tangible acts of love toward others showed me what it means to use everything God has given you to help those in need.

Thank you to my mom and dad by marriage, Doug and Francine Davis. Not only did you allow me to marry your beautiful daughter, but you've also been true parents to me and a beacon of stability in a tumultuous world.

Thank you, Bishop Keith Butler and Pastor Deborah Butler, for growing me up in Christ, teaching me what family life looks like, and giving me a chance in ministry. There are no words to really convey the depth of my gratitude. Word of Faith will always be my home.

To my family at Faith Christian Center and Impact 7 and Beyond—you are the fruit of my labor. Before I had children, I had you. I've watched you grow and seen you blossom. Our best is yet to come. I love each of you with a deep, abiding love.

Joel and Patricia Gregory, thanks for being friends who stick closer than a brother (or sister). And to my siblings by blood and by marriage, you've helped me learn how to put into practice many of the lessons in this book. Thanks for putting up with my "get you there at all costs" mentality. I know my desire for your victory has been radical at times, but it's only because I love you!

Introduction

You've probably heard the saying "Everything happens for a reason." What people often don't realize is that sometimes the reason has nothing to do with the situation at hand and everything to do with your response to it. Life throws us a series of tests. How we handle these tests will determine whether we advance to the next level of increase and promotion God has for us, or if we will remain stagnant where we are right now.

These tests don't arise in our lives because we've done something wrong. In fact, to the contrary, the presence of these tests reveals we've done something right! The enemy, Satan, comes to challenge, prod, and prove us—to see if we really believe what we say we believe.

As the target of Satan's attacks, we will constantly find ourselves in the midst of opposition. After you successfully pass one test and begin seeing an increase in one area, you can't just kick back and say, "Whew! Now I can take it easy." No, my friend, there's always another test around the corner waiting on you.

In fact, I've noticed that tests tend to come in multiples. You may be tested in more than one area at the same time, and both tests will reveal the same thing—whether you will continue to trust God or if you will default to how you used to handle things in your past. The choices you make will determine whether you will receive promotion in God's kingdom, or if you'll have to take the same test over again.

In this book we will look at twelve primary ways we are tested. These tests occur in no particular sequence, and they often overlap one another. All of these tests are reserved for those who are spiritually mature enough to handle them.

In general, God does not initiate these tests. Usually they are initiated by life, but sometimes we initiate them ourselves through choices we make. Our hidden motives can bring on these tests, and so can the hurts we experience in life. Regardless of the cause, the presence of a test indicates that you are up for promotion in the kingdom of God.

Unlike what happens in some school systems, we don't get passed to the next grade until we successfully pass the current test. If we don't stick it out and keep doing things God's way until we see His results, we'll end up coming back around and taking the same test over again—and again and again—until we finally pass.

This is one of the reasons a lot of people live their whole lives frustrated. They don't recognize why those nagging situations keep coming their way. They don't realize they're being tested. Consequently they just think the people on the job don't like them. Or they think everybody is out to get them. Because they don't recognize that they've encountered one of life's tests, they tend to do what comes naturally—they look for a quick way to release the pressure. Oftentimes that means they do something other than what the Bible says to do.

Many times God's way of handling a situation requires us to be patient and wait long enough to see the Word work on the problem. The flesh says, "Just get me out of this right now because it's too uncomfortable! It doesn't feel right! I don't like having to go through this! I don't like having to be patient! I don't like having to wait around for an answer! Even if it won't fix the problem long-term, I want a solution *right now*!"

If you take the easy way out, you'll soon discover that you may have solved one problem today, but that same test is going to come around again. The details will be different, the people involved will be different, but you'll find yourself in exactly the same situation. And each time you make a decision to get out from under the pressure, you unknowingly prevent yourself from going to a higher level spiritually. But if you had just done what the Word says the first time, you'd have passed the test God's way and gone up higher in God.

Let's be honest about this. The reason some people progress spiritually and grow in God, while others stagnate or decline and are always going through problems, is because of the decisions they make. Some people dig into the Word of God and let it lead them through the test while others simply will not allow God to fully renew their minds. Even though both groups may attend the same church, hear the same messages, and lift their hands the same way, when the real pressure comes, some won't make the right choices to follow God's way long enough to see God's results. Consequently they go around and around that same wilderness, and it ends up taking them forty years to go a distance they could have covered in forty days, just like the children of Israel.

This doesn't happen because God likes one person better than the other. It's not because one person is just lucky or had a better start. When you do things God's way long enough, He guarantees to promote you. He would be an unjust God to let you do the right thing for the right amount of time but not let you see any results. The difference is in the choices we make when the heat is on.

HANDLING TEMPTATION THE RIGHT WAY

James 1:12 says, "Blessed is the man that endureth temptation: for when he is tried, he shall receive the crown of life, which the Lord has promised to them that love him." The word *blessed* refers to being prosperous, happy, fortunate, or envied. The word *temptation* means to "put to the proof" through the experience of adversity. This verse tells us that happy, fortunate, to be envied, and prosperous is the man who endures when being put to the proof through the experience of adversity.

The Amplified Bible says, "Blessed (happy, to be envied) is the man who is patient under trial and stands up under temptation, for when he has stood the test and been approved, he will receive [the victor's] crown of life which God has promised to those who love Him." God is letting us know that if we handle our trials and temptations the right way and pass the test, we'll receive the crown of life. We'll get bumped up, promoted, have increase, and experience more spiritual authority than we had before the pressure showed up!

Oftentimes when people are being tested, they ask, "Lord,

what's happening? What am I doing wrong? I'm standing on Your Word. Why don't I see results? What's wrong with me? Is there something I need to know?"

If you have ever found yourself asking these questions, it very well may be that there is nothing wrong with you and that you are on the right track. The answer may be that it's final examination time, and what you are facing is preparation for your next level of promotion and increase.

In the spiritual realm, you don't receive promotion and increase just because you've existed for a long time. Similarly, you won't necessarily be held back just because you're new to the game. God exists outside the boundaries of time, therefore time is not the chief factor He uses when measuring seasons for promotion.

Instead, God allows us to face different life tests that ultimately prove whether we're ready for new levels of spiritual increase. God will allow us to face the same life test over and over and over until we successfully pass it by operating in a manner that is consistent with His Word.

Failure to pass the tests of life can eventually lead to frustration, stagnation, depression, and even quitting. Submitting to God's Word and passing the tests, however, lead to total fulfillment and a life of accomplishment. So learn to recognize the tests of life, and arm yourself to pass them. That is the only way to keep from seeing the same tests again and again.

WE MUST CHOOSE TO PASS THE TEST

One thing you need to know is that these examinations weren't just invented in the last few hundred years. The Bible tells us about individuals who were tested. Some of them passed their tests and some failed.

Abram, later named Abraham, was a man who did both. In Genesis 12 God told Abram to leave his home in Ur of the Chaldees and to depart from his family. Obviously his wife was supposed to go, but everyone else was supposed to stay behind. Yet Abram allowed his emotions and his sense of commitment to his deceased brother cause him to take his nephew, Lot, along with him. And Lot caused Abram all kinds of trouble. Needless to say, Abram flunked that test.

Then Abram went into Egypt and was afraid that the Egyptians were going to take his wife, Sarai, because she was so beautiful. Because she was technically his half-sister, Abram told Sarai to tell the Egyptians that she was his sister. If Abram believed God told him to go to Egypt, then he should have also believed God would keep them alive. Abraham got an F on this test as well.

Later God also told Abram that he would have many descendants even though he was old and still had no children. After Abram and Sarai decided they had waited long enough to have a child, they devised their own plan to have Abram sleep with Sarai's maidservant so she could give him an heir. Yet again problems arose, and Abram failed!

Years later, after Abraham and Sarah miraculously had a son, God gave Abraham another opportunity to pass a test. The Bible says, "And it came to pass after these things, that God did tempt Abraham" (Gen. 22:1). The word *tempt* in this verse comes from the Hebrew word *nacah*, which means "to test, to try, to prove."

Like in the passage in James, it means to put to the proof

or test. So when the Bible says God tempted Abraham, it's not saying that God tried to bait Abraham to do the wrong thing. It means God tried and proved Abraham by putting him to the test.

What was this test? God told Abraham to take his son, Isaac, to a mountain and kill him as a burnt offering unto God. God was asking him to take his son—this miracle child that he waited more than twenty years to have—and sacrifice him. Who would want to obey those instructions? Abraham!

He had gone through so many tests already and had seen the results of flunking them. He was determined to pass this test at all costs.

Abraham wasn't slow to obey God. He got up early the next morning to do what God had said. Abraham knew God's promise to him. He knew that God said his seed would be great in number—more numerous than the sand on the seashore—so God must have had a plan to resurrect his son.

When Abraham reached the top of the mountain, he raised his knife. But before he could plunge it into Isaac, the angel of the Lord called out to him, "Stop! You don't have to do it! There's a ram over there in the bush. Go and sacrifice that ram instead of your son."

God had to test, try, and prove the genuineness of Abraham's faith so he would be qualified to be become the "father of faith," as the apostle Paul explained in Romans 4. (But let me clarify something: God is not calling you to be the father or mother of faith—so if you hear a voice in the middle of the night telling you to go sacrifice your child, that is not God!)

WHY GOD ALLOWS TESTS

God doesn't test us to see if we'll do the wrong thing. He's Alpha and Omega. He knows the end from the beginning. God is *not* the one who puts sickness and disease on people. He doesn't cause people to lack money to pay the rent as a test to see what they'll do.

James 1:13 says, "Let no man say when he is tempted, I am tempted of God: for God cannot be tempted with evil, neither tempteth he any man." Because God can't be tested with evil, He doesn't use evil to test anybody else.

You may run into an obstacle of sickness, but when you do, don't say the Lord brought it upon you. If that's what you think, then you just flunked the test. Instead, go and do what the Bible tells you to do—lay claim to the healing Jesus purchased for you on the cross. Confess God's Word over your body so you can walk in your healing and be strong for the next time you face something like that.

Although He doesn't bring sickness or evil into our lives, God does allow us to encounter the difficulties life brings our way. There are two reasons God does this:

1. So we can demonstrate the genuineness and strength of the faith He has placed inside of us. God wants us to know the quality of what we're made of. When I was a kid, I used to visit my relatives in Arkansas. My cousins there weren't spoiled, big-city kids like I was coming from Detroit. They were rough, tough, and rugged—and I'm not even talking about the boys.

I had to learn how to fight just to protect myself from my girl cousins. I had to toughen up by learning how to go through something without constantly needing to be rescued. In the same way, God allows us to face obstacles so we will toughen up and learn to use the Word He has taught us.

2. So we will be able to handle spiritual promotion. If God is going to promote you and not the person next to you, then there has to be a reason. He doesn't just come along and say, "Well, I like you, and I don't like you." Or, "I'm going to promote you, and I'm not going to promote you." He doesn't tell one person, "I'm going to take you eight levels high," and then tell another, "I'm going to take you only two levels high."

If God did that, He'd be violating His Word. The Bible says God is not a respecter of persons. There has to be some criteria for what qualifies person A to get promoted and not person B. When God tests you, it's not because He doesn't love you. It's not that He wants to see you in discomfort. Oftentimes it's because He wants to prepare you.

When tests come your way, your performance will be a clear indication of where you are spiritually and what level of promotion you can handle. When you step out in faith and see that the Word of God works, you will never again let the enemy make you believe God is not going to be there for you. That is one test you won't have to retake.

NO MORE BABY TACTICS

When we first get saved, God cushions us to help us get through the challenges we face. For example, you may get discouraged one day, and when you open your Bible, you'll turn to scriptures that say, "The Lord is on my side. He will even make a way in the wilderness and rivers in the desert." You'll look up toward the heavens, and the sun will be beaming and the angels singing, and you'll hear the Lord say, "Everything is going to be all right." Or when you get back to your office, the phone will ring and it will be one of your friends, saying, "I don't know what it is, but you're on my heart. So I just called to encourage you and let you know everything will be fine."

But that's early on. After a few years go by, you may find yourself a little discouraged and pick up your Bible, only to open it to a verse that says, "O wretched man that I am." You'll look up, and instead of sunshine, rain will be pouring down. You won't hear a single angel singing. You'll sit at your desk all afternoon and nobody will call. And when you start calling a few people, you'll get their voice mail!

Why doesn't God work the same way? Because once you've been taught what to do, God knows you don't need those little baby tactics to get you through. You've grown and matured. He wants you to be able to handle those irritating situations the right way. You have to rely on what you've been taught from the Word—not only to get you through the period of discouragement but also to help you pass the test and end up completely on top!

If you default, however, and do what your flesh wants to do, the discouragement won't go away. It may disappear for thirty days or six months or two years, but at some point it is going to come right back around. Furthermore, your failure to pass the test is going to cause you to stay stuck where you are—until you get an opportunity for a "do-over."

IS YOUR COMMITMENT GENUINE?

First Timothy 3:8–10 says, "Likewise must the deacons be grave, not doubletongued, not given to much wine, not greedy of filthy lucre; holding the mystery of the faith in a pure conscience. And let these also first be proved."

Proved comes from the Greek word *dokimazo*, which means "to test, to examine, to prove, to scrutinize, to see whether a thing is genuine or not; to recognize as genuine after examination." Before anybody gets promoted to any position in God's kingdom, there's a process they need to go through that will reveal whether their faith walk and commitment is genuine.

You really don't know if your commitment to God is genuine when everything is going well. You find out if God is your rock, your source, your fortress, and your refuge only when adversity shows up. Your flesh may want to turn around and run, but when you're in faith, your spirit man says, "No! We have a new Lord and master now. We have to do this thing completely in accordance with the Word of God!"

MY PRAYER FOR YOU

I wrote this book to help you understand what's going on when obstacles arise in your life. As you read these chapters, I encourage you to keep your heart open to all that God will reveal to you about the tests you have gone through and the tests you will face in the future.

Always keep in mind that each test must be successfully passed in order to proceed to the next phase of promotion and increase that God has predestined for you. It is my prayer that you will not look at these tests begrudgingly or as an encumbrance, but as a steppingstone to greater things in God.

If you could only see the end of what God has in store for

you, you'd know that it's worth going through whatever you have to endure. God has wonderful things planned for your life, and He will prepare you for every step of the way.

Chapter One

The SELF TEST

The Self Test gives believers an opportunity to look into the mirror of love and determine how they rate in comparison to Jesus, who is love personified. Love is not selfish or self-focused. Our Christian walk must be marked by a greater concern for others than ourselves. Every day we spend mired in self-centeredness is another day we miss out on the benefits of our spiritual inheritance.

IT'S FRUSTRATING FOR me as a pastor to pray for the people in my congregation to experience all the benefits of our spiritual inheritance and then not see those blessings manifest in their lives oftentimes. I know the reason they are not walking in the fullness of what God has for them is because they're not mature enough to handle His blessings yet.

I have to remind myself that God is a good father and knows what is best for His children. I am a father, and I love my children with all my heart. But if I had decided to buy them brand-new cars the year my daughter turned ten, my older son turned eight, and my younger son turned four, I would have put them in danger.

I'm sure they would have enjoyed having their own cars, but they weren't mature enough to handle them. They likely would have been hurt or even killed had they tried to use the gifts they had been given.

When you were born again, God released many things to you. You may have felt greater peace, joy, and contentment. Perhaps He healed you of an addiction or freed you from crippling fear. But for all the blessings you received at salvation, there were other things that are part of your inheritance as a child of God that were not released to you. Our Father will be able to give those gifts to you only as you mature spiritually and demonstrate that you are ready to handle them.

We read in 1 Corinthians 13:11, "When I was a child, I talked like a child, I thought like a child, I reasoned like a child; now that I have become a man, I am done with childish ways and have put them aside" (AMP). When babies come out of the womb, they are concerned only with themselves. They don't care if their parents had only two and a half hours of sleep that night. When they're ready to eat, they want to eat—and they will cry until someone feeds them.

Babies don't care if there's an important game on TV. If they're wet, they want to be changed—and they don't want to wait for a commercial. From the moment babies are born, they are self-centered, and children will remain that way until you, as their parent, teach them to be considerate of others. One of the major signs that a child is growing up is when he stops acting out of only self-interest and starts acting in love.

First Corinthians 13 tells us, "Love is patient and kind. Love is not jealous or boastful or proud or rude. It does not demand its own way. It is not irritable, and it keeps no record of being wronged. It does not rejoice about injustice but rejoices whenever the truth wins out. Love never gives up, never loses faith, is always hopeful, and endures through every circumstance. Prophecy and speaking in unknown languages and special knowledge will become useless. But love will last forever!" (vv. 4–8, NLT).

As we mature spiritually, we grow in love; and as we grow in love, we grow in spiritual maturity—which is why *love* is the key to passing *The Self Test*.

The Self Test gives believers an opportunity to look into the mirror of love and determine how they rate in comparison to Jesus, who is love personified. Love is not selfish or self-focused. Our Christian walk must be marked by a greater concern for others than ourselves. Every day we spend mired in self-centeredness is another day we miss out on the benefits of our spiritual inheritance.

The Bible says that our access to our inheritance changes as we mature: "Now what I mean is that as long as the inheritor (heir) is a child and under age, he does not differ from a slave, although he is the master of all the estate" (Gal. 4:1, AMP). In other words, if you belong to Christ, you are Abraham's seed and an heir according to the promise God made to Abraham. But heirs don't receive all the benefits of their inheritance until they grow up enough to show they have the maturity to handle them.

When my son, Kaden, was three years old and getting ready for the K-3 program at our church's school, he had to go through the process of getting potty trained. Every time he would successfully go to the restroom, he would come out dancing and shouting, "I'm going to K-3!"

In the weeks leading up to the first day of school, Kaden would tell everybody, "I'm going to school! I'm going to school! I'm going to school!" He woke up on the first day of school extremely excited: "I'm going to school!" It was the same the second day. But I don't think he factored in his mind that this would continue every day of the week.

On about the fourth or fifth day of school, my wife went to wake Kaden up, and he didn't want to get out of bed. He was no longer excited about K-3. "Kaden, don't you want to go to school?"

"No," he replied. His eyes were still closed.

"No?" she said. "Come on, Kaden. Don't you want to go to school?"

"No."

"Where do you want to go?"

"Disney World!"

Many times that's how it is in our lives. We cry out to God: "Oh, Lord, use me! I'm available to be used by You. Grow me up, Lord. Send me, Lord. Work through me, Lord." Then, as soon as He starts the process of growing us up and getting us ready to be used, we say, "I want to go to Disney World, Lord!"

God does not wait around for people who are not ready to mature. God has a mission to complete. Time is short. He doesn't have time to babysit and placate people who don't really want to grow up. God is ready to use those who are willing to empty themselves out and say, "Lord, whatever You want to do through me, I'm open to being used."

In order to grow up enough to be ready for God's use, you have to empty yourself out and put some of your own plans and thoughts on the shelf. You must be willing to be uncomfortable and go through some things. If you expect to be used by God, you can't be the type of person who is ready to cry and give up at the first sign of trouble.

SELFISH AMBITION

"Let no one say when he is tempted, I am tempted from God; for God is incapable of being tempted by [what is] evil and He Himself tempts no one" (James 1:13, AMP). Occasionally you will find yourself in tests and trials because you allowed your desire to obtain or accomplish something to override what God had planned for you in that season of your life. In fact, if you find yourself pursuing a variety of personal interests instead of what God has ordained for you, you may find yourself experiencing some tests you wouldn't have had to deal with if you'd simply followed the will of God.

A big part of The Self Test is learning how to say no. You must constantly say no to what your flesh wants to do and say yes to the will of God. This includes the obvious sins— fornication, cursing, murder, cheating, stealing—as well as some things that are not necessarily categorized as a sin. It may not be wrong to go back to school or pursue a business venture, but if that is not God's will for you right now, you will have to say no.

There are some things that are good and that God does want you to pursue, but it may not be His will for you to go after them now. So saying no can mean you're going to submit to what God wants for you in that season of your life instead of what you want for yourself.

For example, I've known people who wanted a new house so badly they were willing to pursue it at all costs. They refused to give financially to God so they could purchase the home, and they ignored common sense. They would add up every dime from the husband's and the wife's income, then consider about 286 banks in search of a lender willing to manipulate the numbers to give them a loan at some ridiculous interest rate.

They'd be "approved" all right, but the problem is, they manipulated the system to get something God really didn't want them to have just yet. Consequently there would be no grace from God to help pay for that house, and they'd end up in a financial jam every month. They'd always have more month than money. This would also put them in a spiritual dilemma. They'd have to decide, "Do I pay this house note, or do I give to God?"

Where did this big mess come from? Self-interest. They were saying, "I want this house *right now*. I deserve this house *right now*." Again, it's not that God doesn't want us to have a house—He wants us to have all good things to enjoy—but there's a right time and a right way for everything.

In like manner I've seen people pursue cars, clothes, boats, jobs, and many other things at any cost. They will go into debt, maxing out their credit cards, yet not have anything to show for it because everything they bought had no genuine value. Most of us know we must seek God about the big stuff like discovering what He's called us to do. But sometimes we fail to realize God wants us to get rid of *all* of our self-interest, even in the small things. The Bible says, "In all your ways, know, recognize, and acknowledge Him" (Prov. 3:6, AMP).

Everything we have must be dedicated to the King of kings and the Lord of lords. And when He comes knocking on our door, instructing us to use what we have for the kingdom or to give it away, we must be ready to release it immediately. We can't hold on to anything God has put in our hands; we must be willing to give it away for kingdom purposes. If we have a gift, talent, or resource in our hands and we won't use it to advance the kingdom, that is a clear sign that we are allowing our self-interest to determine our actions instead of God.

THE FAST WAY OUT

Self-interest and self-pursuit have destroyed many things God intended to be blessings in our lives. A lot of marriages have broken up because of selfishness. Spouses became so consumed with what they wanted that they ignored the needs of their partner. Parents have become estranged from their children because they put their dreams and ambitions over the needs of their family.

We may wonder, "How could that have happened?" But it could happen to any of us if we allow our own selfish desires to override what God wants done in our lives. We can pass The Self Test, Jesus tells us, when we stop being so focused on our own needs.

> Therefore I tell you, stop being perpetually uneasy (anxious and worried) about your life, what you shall eat or what you shall drink; or about your body, what you shall put on. Is not life greater [in quality] than

food, and the body [far above and more excellent] than clothing? Look at the birds of the air; they neither sow nor reap nor gather into barns, and yet your heavenly Father keeps feeding them. Are you not worth much more than they?

And who of you by worrying and being anxious can add one unit of measure (cubit) to his stature or to the span of his life? And why should you be anxious about clothes? Consider the lilies of the field and learn thoroughly how they grow; they neither toil nor spin. Yet I tell you, even Solomon in all his magnificence (excellence, dignity, and grace) was not arrayed like one of these.

But if God so clothes the grass of the field, which today is alive and green and tomorrow is tossed into the furnace, will He not much more surely clothe you, O you of little faith? Therefore do not worry and be anxious, saying, What are we going to have to eat? or, What are we going to have to drink? or, What are we going to have to wear? For the Gentiles (heathen) wish for and crave and diligently seek all these things, and your heavenly Father knows well that you need them all. But seek (aim at and strive after) first of all His kingdom and His righteousness (His way of doing and being right), and then all these things taken together will be given you besides.

—MATTHEW 6:25–33, AMP

God doesn't want us living with a self-focused mentality. He tells us, "Don't even take any thought about what you're going to eat. Don't be consumed with concerns about what you're going to wear. Don't worry about what you're going to drive or where you're going to live."

People of this world often become concerned about what they have on, or impressing somebody with the car they drive, or feeling good about themselves because they live in a certain neighborhood. But the moment we get consumed with our desires, we've flunked The Self Test. Remember, if we flunk this test, we're going to have to take it all over again.

The fastest way to get out of the kindergarten level of spiritual maturity is to do what Jesus says: "Seek first the kingdom of God." Stop focusing on what you need or want. Take your requests to the throne of God. Pray about it and then leave it at the altar. Get busy doing what the Lord told you to do. Then you'll pass The Self Test and get promoted to the next assignment.

Jesus operated this way. He was not self-focused. He was not consumed with self-interest. Instead, He always had the plan of God on His mind, which was to minister to other people. He said, "For I came down from heaven, not to do mine own will, but the will of him that sent me" (John 6:38).

I wonder what would happen if more believers were consumed with doing the will of God more than they were with fulfilling their own desires. What if more Christians put ministering to others before their personal schedules? What if they made ministry a priority instead of squeezing it in after they did everything for themselves?

Could it be that your choice whether to help at your local church and give some of your personal time is your Self Test? Could it be that God really wants to show you that your service to the kingdom is more important than what *you* want to do with your time? God has so much in store for you, but you have to be ready to receive it.

POWER FOR PROMOTION

It's frustrating to see people continually come to church and just *shout* about inheriting the promises of God. It's time for them to begin *receiving* the promises! It's not enough to say riches are stored up for the just. It's time for the just to start possessing the riches of their inheritance in Christ—and that won't happen until they pass The Self Test.

Remember, God won't just throw you in the game. He'll wait until your due season. It could be that failing to pass The Self Test has disqualified you for promotion. If you're too good to do the small and humbling jobs God might place on your heart to do—such as helping to clean the church or serving as a parking attendant—then maybe you're not ready to preach from the pulpit either.

Are you going to put your own desires ahead of the will of God? Are you going to let what you want to do, what you feel, what you're going through become more important than what God has ordained for your life right now? If so, that might mean you're failing The Self Test.

Fortunately, God gives us the grace—the supernatural power—we need to overcome our selfishness.

> But He gives us more and more grace (power of the Holy Spirit, to meet this evil tendency and all others fully). That is why He says, God sets Himself against the proud and haughty, but gives grace [continually] to the lowly (those who are humble enough to receive it).
> —JAMES 4:6, AMP

The word *more* in this verse is used in the continual sense: "He gives us more and more and more and more of the grace and power of the Holy Spirit to fully meet this evil tendency." What evil tendency is the Word of God speaking of? It's the tendency to become self-focused. There is a grace God gives that will allow you to not focus on you.

Are you a selfish person? To find out, don't go look at yourself in the mirror and say, "Self, dost thou thinketh thou art a selfish person?" The best way to know if you come across as selfish is to ask the people around you. Ask your family members, your friends, and your coworkers. They will tell you.

If you are a selfish person, you cannot just say, "Well, I'm going to stop being selfish." You have to trust God to give you what you need to conquer this evil tendency. Then, when selfish tendencies try to rise up, this grace from God will manifest, empowering you to focus on somebody else's need instead of your own.

But you have to be willing to yield to that grace because the Bible says it comes only on the humble. You must be willing to search your own heart and then yield to the power of God so He can help you.

> Let nothing be done through strife or vainglory; but in lowliness of mind let each esteem other better than themselves. Look not every man on his own things, but every man also on the things of others. Let this mind be in you, which was also in Christ Jesus: Who, being in the form of God, thought it not robbery to be equal with God: But made himself of no reputation,

and took upon him the form of a servant, and was
made in the likeness of men.

—Philippians 2:3–7

Notice the attitude portrayed here. This passage is basically
saying, "Don't get consumed with your own needs, but become
consumed with the needs of others." When you pass The Self
Test, it means you've stopped focusing on yourself and you've
taken on the attitude of a servant. A servant is not interested
in getting credit. A servant doesn't care if he receives a pat on
the back.

A bona fide servant is happy just knowing he was able to be
a blessing to the person he was serving. Ultimately, the One
we are serving is God Almighty. Take on the heart of a true
servant, and you will find The Self Test an easy one to
pass every time.

DISCUSSION STARTERS

1. How does The Self Test help us inherit the promises of God?

2. How can seeking after a good thing end up being a bad thing?

3. Do you show signs of selfishness? Ask those who know you best if you show signs of selfishness. Give them permission to be honest with you. Be sure to let them know there will be no retaliation.

4. What actions steps can you take to pass The
   Self Test? Write them down and keep them on
   hand.

Chapter Two

The TIME TEST

The purpose of The Time Test is to give the person being tested an opportunity to grow in faith. God wants us to learn to trust Him for His timing and provision instead of manipulating the outcome to fit our current state of immaturity.

W<small>E ALL WANT</small> what God has for us—and we want it right now! You know how it is after you've just started believing God for something. Perhaps you've been in a church service and have gotten excited about something God said He was going to do in your life. You dance, you shout, and you rejoice! You are determined to keep believing for that promise to come to pass—however long it may take!

But a few weeks go by. Then a few months. Before long a year has passed—and the thing you were believing for still hasn't come to pass. What the flesh tends to do at this point is to get discouraged. This is because we hate waiting. That's just human nature. We hate waiting in line. We hate waiting in traffic. We hate waiting for anything.

So with every day that passes, your flesh starts telling you that what you're believing for isn't going to happen. And then—because you really do want what God promised—you begin to think, "What can *I* do to fix this? How can *I* make it happen?"

A lot of people have made their situations worse because they came up with their own plans to fix their problems. In their heads that little clock was ticking, and their minds started to tell them God might not come through. So instead of being patient enough to wait for God's best, they settled for less.

Sometimes God will allow us to face certain situations to show us we *have* to wait for Him. This is what I call *The Time Test*.

Galatians 6:9 says, "And let us not be weary in well doing: for in due season we shall reap, if we faint not." The Amplified Bible says it this way: "And let us not lose heart and grow weary and faint in acting nobly and doing right, for in due time and at the appointed season we shall reap, if we do not loosen and relax our courage and faint."

The purpose of The Time Test is to give the person being tested an opportunity to grow in faith. God wants us to learn to trust Him for His timing and provision instead of manipulating the outcome to fit our current state of immaturity.

There is only one question on The Time Test: "Will you be patient long enough to allow God to work out your situation in His timing, or will you resort to your own way of doing things because you don't want to wait?"

The Time Test is designed to teach us that we have to start using our faith to get us into our due season. We can't try to make something happen in our own strength simply because we want an answer right now.

IS LIFE PASSING YOU BY?

Single person, will you wait for God to send you His choice as your mate? Or will you listen to your flesh screaming, "I want somebody! I want to be with somebody! I'm tired of being by myself! I feel like life is passing me by"?

It's so sad when people flunk The Time Test in the area of relationships. They reach out and grab somebody just so they won't be alone, then find themselves married to Mr. Right Now when Mr. Right finally walks by. Then they're mad as fire!

Instead, if you're single you could decide to pass The Time Test by being patient. You could keep working on yourself while you're waiting. You could keep doing all the things God has been talking with you about instead of telling yourself, "I've got to be in a relationship right now!"

Have you noticed that whatever you've been waiting for seems to show up faster when you get busy? Say you're at home waiting for someone to pick you up. If you're at the front door looking out the window and checking your watch every two minutes, it will seem like they're taking forever. However, if you get up and start cleaning the house, put a load of clothes in the washing machine, and take care of other chores, the person will seem to show up in no time.

While you're keeping busy, the person you've been waiting for rings the doorbell or blows the horn. You end up having to scamper to get out the door! It takes the same amount of time either way, but it doesn't feel as long when you're not sitting around preoccupied with how long you're waiting.

David knew the importance of waiting for God's appointed time. He wrote these words while fleeing King Saul, who was trying to kill him: "My times are in thy hand: deliver me from the hand of mine enemies, and from them that persecute me" (Ps. 31:15).

Obviously David wanted deliverance right away. But notice that before he asked God to manifest His victory, David said, "My time is in Your hand, God." Then he said, "Of course, I'd like to have the victory right now, but I'm willing to wait as long as I need to. I'm giving this situation to You. I put the timing in Your hands. Work this out in the time You know is right for me."

The Message Bible says it this way: "Hour by hour I place my days in your hand, safe from the hands out to get me." Every single hour of the day we can say, as David did, "God, I give this hour to You." The moment we start trying to put all the pieces together and figure out what we're going to be doing five years from now, ten years from now, fifteen years from now, that's when the pressure shows up.

This is especially true of single women. Everybody starts telling you, "You're in your thirties now. You have only a few more years to still have children." That's pressure!

I'm not saying this is easy to deal with. I'm a man. I have no idea how tough it is mentally to face this reality. But you must still understand this, young lady—it's even tougher to face the consequences of rushing out and jumping ahead of God!

With The Time Test we learn that if we try to rush things, all we end up doing is jumping out of one pot of pressure into another. That won't solve the problem. The situation will only get fixed when we slow down, trust God, and continue doing His will until we see the victory manifest.

If you rush ahead of God and try to make things happen on your own, you may get married and have children but have to raise those children by yourself because the marriage didn't work out. What's age to God, anyway? Sarah was ninety years old when she gave birth to Isaac. I know you're not planning to have children when you're ninety, but you must have that level of commitment to wait on the Lord's timing. You must be determined to pass The Time Test and not jump ahead of God. If you get ahead of God, you'll find yourself in worse trouble later on.

EVERYTHING HAS A SEASON

Ecclesiastes 3:1–8 tells us, "To every thing there is a season, and a time to every purpose under the heaven: A time to be born, and a time to die; a time to plant, and a time to pluck up that which is planted; a time to kill, and a time to heal; a time to break down, and a time to build up; a time to weep, and a time to laugh; a time to mourn, and a time to dance; a time to cast away stones, and a time to gather stones together; a time to embrace, and a time to refrain from embracing; a time to get, and a time to lose; a time to keep, and a time to cast away; a time to rend, and a time to sew; a time to keep silence, and a time to speak; a time to love, and a time to hate; a time of war, and a time of peace."

No matter how much we try to manipulate things to make this the appointed season for our promise to manifest, we can't rush things if we're waiting for God's anointing and sanction.

No matter how big a hurry we may be in, God is not going to hasten things along. He waits until the timing is right.

Galatians 4:4 says God sent forth His Son in "the fullness of the time." Think about that for a moment. Don't you know that God could have brought Jesus on the scene through Sarah? He could have called Sarah to be the virgin who gave birth to His Son. But God has a perfect time for everything. If He waited for the right time to redeem the world, you'd better believe He's going to wait for the right season to manifest whatever you're believing for. You just need to be willing to wait for His perfect timing and trust Him.

We all have seasons in our lives. When it's your season, you will bring forth good fruit, and nobody can stop the flow of God's anointing on your life except you. I like to say, "When it's on you, it's just on you."

People can be mad at you. They can dislike you. They can be jealous because you were promoted. But so what? When God promotes, there's nothing anybody can do about it. God doesn't ask permission. All He asks is that you be patient and pass The Time Test—just be in the right place at the right time, and be doing what He told you to do.

FLUNKING THE TIME TEST

Don't be like Abraham when he was waiting for the child God promised. God told him to look at the stars in the sky and the sand on the seashore because that was how numerous his seed was going to be. Abraham was seventy-five years old when God first came to him and made this promise.

We might ask, "Why didn't God do it right then? If Abraham fathered a baby at seventy-five years of age, wouldn't that be enough of a miracle?" Evidently Abraham wasn't ready to receive the promise of God.

He left Ur of the Chaldees and flunked the first test coming out of the gate because he took Lot with him when God told him to leave his family. Then when he went into Egypt, he flunked another test because he was afraid God didn't have enough power to protect him. It's clear that Abraham wasn't ready for his promise to manifest yet.

Eleven years after God promised Abraham he would be the father of many nations, he still had no child. Then Sarah came up with a grand idea. "We don't have a child yet and we've been trying," she says. "So why don't you take my young Egyptian servant, Hagar, and sleep with her, and then when she gives birth, we'll take that baby as our child. Maybe that's what the Lord intended."

Abraham, being the great man of faith that he was, says, "Good idea!"

So he took Hagar as his wife and lay with her, and she became pregnant. But after Hagar conceived, she began to feel superior to Sarah and started to mock her. So Sarah did what every woman has the prerogative to do—she changed her mind.

Sarah told Abraham to get Hagar out of the compound. Abraham was eighty-six years old at this time. Remember, when we flunk The Time Test by trying to make things happen ourselves, not only do we have to take the same test again, but we also delay the process.

Abraham was ninety-nine years old when he was given another shot at The Time Test. Thirteen years of this man's life went by because he went ahead of God and tried to bring the promise to pass in his own timing. Abraham and Sarah tried to manipulate the situation because they felt God wasn't moving fast enough.

Abraham had to wait because he needed to work out some internal issues. He had to learn to trust God, and that lack of faith was causing the manifestation of his promise to be delayed. If he had dealt with those heart issues when he was seventy-five or eighty, God may have given him Isaac back then. As it turned out, it took thirteen years of nothing happening before Abraham was finally ready to listen.

God came along and told Abraham, "No longer am I going to do all of the work, but now you're going to come into covenant with Me. You're going to circumcise the flesh of your foreskin, as well as that of your son and servants, as a reminder that you owe Me something in return. I'm counting on you to not mess up what I'm trying to do in your life."

When Abraham finally comes into covenant with God, it takes only three months for him and Sarah to conceive. The next year, Isaac is born. Why was Sarah able to get pregnant then when she hadn't been able to conceive all those years? Abraham passed the test! How did he pass the test? The circumcision in his flesh kept reminding him, "Whoa, whoa, whoa! I have a part to play in this covenant relationship. I can't rush out and do it ahead of God."

That's why Abraham was ready to obey when God told him to take his son to the top of the mountain. (See Genesis 22.) He had flunked enough tests. He was tired of failing. I don't know about you, but that's true for me as well. I have flunked too many tests in my life, and I'm tired of failing. Like Abraham, now I only want to get it right!

RECEIVING GOD'S BEST

Do you want to pass The Time Test? It may not be easy, but it's simple. Every day you just need to open up your heart to hear what the Lord is saying to you. Look at the decisions you may be getting ready to make, and be sure you're not making a choice now that you'll regret years later.

If you don't have total peace, which only God can provide, that may be because you're not operating in God's timing. Submit your way to the Lord and receive His best. God's best is so much better than what you can dream up on your very best day!

So just wait on God. Tell yourself, "If it's not quite, it's not right." If you find yourself trying to manipulate the situation to make it happen, it's not God's best. You're jumping the gun. Slow down and just be patient.

Get up every day, do what God is telling you to do for that day, and trust Him. Do what He has appointed you to do, and in due season, if you faint not, you shall have your heart's desire. If you're ready to put your times in God's hands, make this your prayer:

Thank You, Lord, for giving me understanding and helping me to realize why I've been stuck in some places longer than I thought I should be. Thank You for helping me understand why certain things haven't worked out the way I know they should have. Thank You for helping me to get further clarity.

The enemy is just trying to get me to jump the gun and move outside of Your timing. Today I have purposed in my heart to take my time. I'm going to trust Your timing and believe that You know how to work the situation out far better than I do. Even if it looks like my way could work, I'm willing to trust You, because doing what is ultimately the best before You is what I live for. Thank You for giving me the grace to be patient and pass The Time Test. I give You praise and glory for this lesson learned, in Jesus's name. Thank You, Lord God. Amen!

DISCUSSION STARTERS

1. Can you think of a time when you had to wait on God? Did you pass or fail the test?

2. Think of a time when you failed The Time Test. How did it affect your life?

3. Is there something God has instructed you to do while you're waiting for His promise?

Chapter Three

The PRESSURE TEST

The Pressure Test will reveal whether affliction or persecution will cause you to seek refuge, consolation, or relief from any god other than the Most High God. The Pressure Test challenges the true commitment of your heart. It will expose whether your love for God is a mere matter of convenience or if you will bless the Lord at all times.

THERE ISN'T A person alive who doesn't face some pressure. Pressure doesn't have to get the best of you, but it will always be there. Whether you have a great job or are unemployed, you're going to feel pressure. Whether you're married or single, whether you have children or not, you're going to feel pressure. Whether you're male or female, tall or short, black or white, Hispanic, Asian, Indian, Jamaican, or African, you're going to feel pressure.

After noticing that even those who I believed were strong

in their faith often dealt with pressure in unhealthy ways, I asked God why. I believe I have been shown some things that will be a benefit and a blessing to you, and that will help you learn how to handle pressure the right way. Let's talk about *The Pressure Test.*

The Pressure Test will reveal whether affliction or persecution will cause you to seek refuge, consolation, or relief from any god other than the Most High God. The Pressure Test challenges the true commitment of your heart. It will expose whether your love for God is a mere matter of convenience or if you will bless the Lord at all times.

Jesus told us, "These things I have spoken unto you, that in me ye might have peace. In the world ye shall have tribulation: but be of good cheer; I have overcome the world" (John 16:33). The word *peace* in this verse comes from the Greek word *eirēnē*, which corresponds to the Hebrew word *shalom* and means completeness, soundness, nothing missing, and nothing broken.

In Jesus we can have completeness and soundness with nothing missing and nothing broken in our lives. Praise God for that! However, you can't just pay attention to the first part of the verse and ignore the rest.

Jesus goes on to promise us that we will have tribulation. He didn't say in the world you *might* have tribulation. He didn't say in the world there's a strong possibility you'll have tribulation. He didn't say in the world, if you do things the wrong way, you'll have tribulation. He said if you are living in the world, you can take it to the bank: tribulation will show up.

There is tribulation that will come your way whether you're doing the right thing or the wrong thing. I know you'd rather not have to acknowledge that fact. But the reality is that it's in the Bible, and it is going to come to pass whether you like it or not.

The word *tribulation* comes from a Greek word *thlipsis*, which literally means *pressure*. So when Jesus says "in the world you shall have tribulation," what He's actually saying is *in the world you shall have pressure*. There's not a person alive who is able to live life without it. Because Jesus took the time to make such a direct statement about the pressure we will face in this life, it behooves us to learn how to deal with it.

The apostle Paul was a perfect example of how we should deal with pressure-filled situations. He ran into more trouble than anybody I know of. He was beaten with rods multiple times, stoned, and shipwrecked. He was often hungry and thirsty. He had trouble with bandits, with his own people, and even with the Gentiles he was sent to minister to. Yet consider his words:

> And now, behold, I go bound in the spirit unto Jerusalem, not knowing the things that shall befall me there: Save that the Holy Ghost witnesseth in every city, saying that bonds and afflictions abide me. *But none of these things move me*, neither count I my life dear unto myself, so that I might finish my course with joy, and the ministry, which I have received of the Lord Jesus, to testify the gospel of the grace of God.
> —ACTS 20:22–24, EMPHASIS ADDED

Throughout his many hardships Paul always maintained an attitude that said, "None of these things are going to move me." Paul understood that he had a mission and assignment from God, and if he backed down and cowered because of the pressure, he would not be able to obtain all that the kingdom of God had to offer him.

Many people don't deal with pressure the way Paul did. I've seen some people drink alcohol or use drugs when they're under pressure. Getting drunk or high allows them to escape the reality of what they're facing. However, when they come out of that high or drunken state, the problem is still there—and it may even be worse because of what they did or said while intoxicated.

Some people who don't deal well with pressure can't sleep. Others develop ulcers. Some lash out at other people—just say the simplest thing, and they're ready to bite your head off! Other people get up in the middle of the night and grab a bucket of Kentucky Fried Chicken with biscuits, honey, and mashed potatoes to comfort them. When the pressure is off, however, they complain because they're five pounds heavier. Then there are those who don't eat at all when the pressure hits.

Some people respond to pressure in their life by becoming extremely depressed. They disappear for days at a time. They watch the caller ID when friends and family are trying to call. It's not that they dislike the people who are calling; it's simply too much for them to communicate with someone while they're under the weight of that pressure.

Some people lie when they're under pressure. Even some Christians, if backed into a corner, will come up with a fast lie. Once they tell one lie, they have to tell another one to back up the first one—and before you know it, they're wrapped up in a whole web of deceit just because they were afraid to deal with the pressure the right way.

Many people develop a running spirit when they're under pressure. They'll go from city to city, church to church, job to job, relationship to relationship—running away at the first sign of pressure. They don't realize that there is nowhere on earth you can run from pressure.

LET GOD'S LOVE SATURATE YOUR HEART

If you're going to successfully pass The Pressure Test, the first thing you have to do is let God's love saturate your heart. I know this seems elementary because you already know God loves you. But if you really have a revelation of how much He loves you, then no matter what tribulation the enemy tries to bring your way, that pressure will not peel you away from your loving Father and make you run away from Him.

The Bible says, "Who shall separate us from the love of Christ? shall tribulation, or distress, or persecution, or famine, or nakedness, or peril, or sword?...Nay, in all these things we are more than conquerors through him that loved us. For I am persuaded, that neither death, nor life, nor angels, nor principalities, nor powers, nor things present, nor things to come, nor height, nor depth, nor any other creature, shall be able to separate us from the love of God, which is in Christ Jesus our Lord" (Rom. 8:35, 37–39).

Let this fact saturate your heart until it becomes all you think about when trouble shows up. Saturating your heart with the Word of God is like marinating your food rather than just seasoning it. If you sprinkle some seasonings on top of the meat you're getting ready to prepare, the flavor just sits on the outside. But if you marinate the meat for a while, the flavor gets down deep and every bite is infused.

You need to take the time to marinate in the love of God so you can deal with the pressures that show up in your life. When you have a revelation of how much God loves you, it takes the pressure off of you and puts it back on His love.

BE COURAGEOUS

The second thing you must do to pass The Pressure Test is choose to operate in courage when under pressure. The Bible says, "And we have known and believed the love that God hath to us. God is love; and he that dwelleth in love dwelleth in God, and God in him. Herein is our love made perfect, that *we may have boldness in the day of judgment*: because as he is, so are we in this world" (1 John 4:16–17, emphasis added).

The "day of judgment" is not just when you stand before God to give an account of the deeds you've done while on the earth. The "day of judgment" is the day of test, trial, and temptation in your life. Knowing God loves us and we love Him gives us confidence that we can overcome anything that shows up in our lives.

It's like when my younger brother would mouth off at kids who were older—and bigger—than he was. He wasn't afraid because he knew that I, being his older brother, would defend him. Sometimes boys who were bigger than me would pick on my brother. Even though I was scared, I knew that if we wanted to live in peace and not have to deal with those bullies again, I was going to have to stand up to them. You can't let the devil think that every time he brings pressure your way you're going to quit or run.

The moment you let the devil think he's running the show, he will push you around, always telling you what you can and cannot do. So you just need to rise up and declare, "I will not be pushed around by pressure. I will not be bullied because the Lord loves me." You won't be afraid of what may come toward you when you have a clear revelation of the love God has for you. First John 4:18 tells us, "There is no fear in love; but perfect love casteth out fear."

Courage is not the absence of fear, someone once said. Rather, it is being terrified but willing to keep persevering anyway. If you had no fear coming against you, there would be no need for courage. Deciding to operate in courage means you're not going to let the contrary circumstance get the best of you. Even if you can't see how things are going to work out, it means you're going to keep walking forward.

The Bible tells of a woman who heard about Jesus and decided to be courageous and go and see Him.

> And, behold, a woman, which was diseased with an issue of blood twelve years, came behind him, and touched the hem of his garment: For she said within herself, If I may but touch his garment, I shall be whole. But Jesus turned him about, and when he saw her, he said, Daughter, be of good comfort; thy faith hath made thee whole. And the woman was made whole from that hour.
>
> —MATTHEW 9:20–22

When this woman showed up in the crowd, she was taking a chance that somebody might point her out and say she had no business being out among the people. She was ceremonially unclean according to Levitical law and could have been stoned to death before she ever got to Jesus. Just like this woman, if you're going to put the pressure on your pressure instead of it putting the pressure on you, you have to make a decision to operate in courage. Taking a bold, courageous step could be exactly what's needed to turn your situation around.

Joshua was another person in the Bible who had to learn to be courageous in times of great pressure. When Moses died and he was chosen to lead the children of Israel, Joshua had to step into big shoes. Four times God had to instruct him to have courage. But God didn't just tell him to be courageous without also telling him how to do it. God said, "Be strong and of a good courage; be not afraid, neither be thou dismayed: *for the* LORD *thy God is with thee whithersoever thou goest*" (Josh. 1:9, emphasis added).

You have no reason to be dismayed by the circumstances you're facing because the Lord your God is with you! He said He will never leave you or forsake you (Heb. 13:5). Have confidence in His promise to be with you and refuse to fear.

RECOGNIZE THE POWER OF PATIENCE

The next thing you must do to pass The Pressure Test is learn to be patient in tribulation. The Bible says, "Rejoice and exult in hope; be steadfast and patient in suffering and tribulation; be constant in prayer" (Rom. 12:12, AMP).

The word *patient* here comes from a Greek word that means "to endure, bear bravely, and calmly." It literally means "to abide under," which means to continue living the same despite your circumstance.

Don't let the devil dictate what you're going to do; stay the same and be constant in the things God has instructed you to do. Sometimes people think that patience means sitting back on the sideline and just waiting for something to happen. That's not the kind of patience the Bible instructs us to have. Biblical patience is when you remain in faith and continue to obey God despite what the enemy tries to bring your way.

If you want to take hold of the promises of God, you need to be patient. The Bible says, "Cast not away therefore your confidence, which hath great recompence of reward. For ye have need of patience, that, after ye have done the will of God, ye might receive the promise" (Heb. 10:35–36). Even if what you see is contrary to what you want, keep getting up every day praising God. Keep a smile on your face.

Hebrews 6:12–15 tells us that through faith and patience we will inherit the promises of God. As long as you continue doing the things God has told you to do, refusing to be moved by the pressure the enemy is bringing your way, you will receive what the kingdom of God has for you.

ADJUST YOUR PERSPECTIVE

The next step we must take to pass The Pressure Test is to refuse to give the pressure we're facing more credit than it deserves. The apostle Paul wrote, "For which cause we faint not; but though our outward man perish, yet the inward man is renewed day by day. For our light affliction, which is but for a moment, worketh for us a far more exceeding and eternal weight of glory" (2 Cor. 4:16–17).

As we've already discussed, Paul's life was not smooth sailing all the time. But Paul called the afflictions he faced "light." It's clear that he had a different mind-set than most people have.

No matter how tough your situation, you can't afford to magnify it. The larger you make the problem, the harder it's going to be for you to overcome it. You need to daily declare that your God is bigger than your problem. There is nothing too difficult for Him.

When you begin to magnify the Lord and declare His greatness, you'll see that the weight of the pressure becomes lighter and lighter and lighter. It may not be because the situation has changed but because your perspective has changed now that you're focusing on almighty God rather than your problem.

CHOOSE THE JOY OF THE LORD

Another thing you need to do to pass The Pressure Test is decide to laugh at the devil despite the pressure you face. Paul said, "I am filled with comfort, I am exceeding joyful in all our tribulation" (2 Cor. 7:4). Paul was sure to laugh in the midst of his pressure. Why? Because he was confident in the fact that God would see him through it all. As he magnified God, he came to realize that Satan is not as powerful as he tries to make himself out to be.

Isaiah 14:12–17 says: "How art thou fallen from heaven, O Lucifer, son of the morning! how art thou cut down to the ground, which didst weaken the nations! For thou hast said in thine heart, I will ascend into heaven, I will exalt my throne above the stars of God: I will sit also upon the mount of the congregation, in the sides of the north: I will ascend above the heights of the clouds; I will be like the most High. Yet thou shalt be brought down to hell, to the sides of the pit. They that see thee shall narrowly look upon thee, and consider thee, saying, Is this the man that made the earth to tremble, that did shake kingdoms; that made the world as a wilderness, and destroyed the cities thereof; that opened not the house of his prisoners?"

When we actually see Satan, we're going to be surprised by how small and powerless he really is. People give the devil way too much credit. Don't give Satan—or the pressure he's trying to bring your way—any more credit than it deserves because our God is still an awesome God. Don't allow what you see or what others say about the situation cause you to become afraid. Have faith in your covenant with God just as David did when he fought against and defeated Goliath. Run at your pressure with a heart full of faith!

The Word of God tells us in James 1:2: "Count it all joy when ye fall into divers temptations." One day my wife, April, and I were in the car when we received a phone call with some really bad news about someone we care about. It was such bad news that my emotions were tempted to go down, but I'd been meditating on this verse in James for a while. So I said to April, "Let's laugh."

While we were driving down the expressway, we started saying, "Ha, ha, ha." It was just as dry as dry can be. My mind said, "This is stupid and you look stupid! People driving past probably think you're crazy."

But I kept doing it. "Ha, ha, ha, ha." Between laughs my mind wanted to go back to thinking about the bad news I had just received. Instead I set my mind to count it all joy and kept laughing. We had not even driven one mile when the anointing kicked in! Now I was concerned because I was laughing hysterically and still needed to control the car. By the time we exited the highway, we were totally set free! What's the moral of this story? It doesn't matter how you feel. Go ahead and laugh at the devil. Ha, ha, ha, ha!

I'm not telling you to do anything that God Himself doesn't do. Psalm 37:12–13 tells us, "The wicked plot against the [uncompromisingly] righteous (the upright in right standing with God); they gnash at them with their teeth. *The Lord laughs at [the wicked]*, for He sees that their own day [of defeat] is coming" (AMP, emphasis added). That's all you're doing. You're laughing at the devil because you can see that things are not going to end the way he thinks they will.

MAKE TRUST YOUR FOUNDATION

If you want to pass The Pressure Test, you also must make a decision to trust in God. The Bible says, "Trust in the LORD with all thine heart; and lean not unto thine own understanding. In all thy ways acknowledge him, and he shall direct thy paths" (Prov. 3:5–6). If we don't make a firm commitment to trust God, then we'll find ourselves letting the pressure overtake our lives.

Trusting God can't just be something we say out of our mouths. It must be something we do. People may say they trust God, but that doesn't necessarily mean they trust Him.

Psalm 55:22 in the Amplified Bible says, "Cast your burden on the Lord [releasing the weight of it] and He will sustain you; He will never allow the [consistently] righteous to be moved (made to slip, fall, or fail)." Give your problems over to Him and allow Him to bear the weight of the pressure for you. You can trust Him to bring you out on the other side victorious.

Psalm 62:8 says, "Trust in him at all times; ye people, pour out your heart before him: God is a refuge for us. Selah."

Selah means *pause and calmly think* about what you just read or heard. What a wonderful thing for us to stop and think about—God is a refuge for us. We can run to the safety of God's presence, and He will protect us there. There is not a person alive who can keep you safe from *all* harm, but God can. Your parents, spouse, best friend—none of them can do what God can do. Trust in Him to do it for you today!

RUN TO THE SECRET PLACE

One final thing you must do to pass The Pressure Test is decide to abide in the secret place.

> He that dwelleth in the secret place of the most High shall abide under the shadow of the Almighty. I will say of the LORD, He is my refuge and my fortress: my God; in him will I trust. Surely he shall deliver thee from the snare of the fowler, and from the noisome pestilence. He shall cover thee with his feathers, and under his wings shalt thou trust: his truth shall be thy shield and buckler. Thou shalt not be afraid for the terror by night; nor for the arrow that flieth by day; nor for the pestilence that walketh in darkness; nor for the destruction that wasteth at noonday. A thousand shall fall at thy side, and ten thousand at thy right hand; but it shall not come nigh thee. Only with thine eyes shalt thou behold and see the reward of the wicked. Because thou hast made the LORD, which is my refuge, even the most High, thy habitation; there shall no evil befall thee, neither shall any plague come nigh thy dwelling.
>
> —PSALM 91:1–10

God's protection and deliverance are blessings that stem from abiding in the secret place of God's presence. When you abide in the secret place, times of pressure won't feel so heavy anymore because you'll be with Him.

Not everyone will take the time to enter the secret place. Some people just won't get away from all the distractions in order to get there. But if you do what it takes to get before God and press into that secret place, you'll find His protection and power.

One of the best ways to enter into God's presence is through worship. This can be done in a public service, of course, but worship is a personal thing between you and God. Genuine worship requires you to think and talk about who God is instead of focusing on what you're going through.

It's not pleasing to God when we allow pressure to overtake us. He doesn't want us to let it bombard our minds and control our actions. But when God sees us step up and act upon His Word despite what we're going through, that makes Him smile. When we submit our daily life decisions to God's Word, that is worship that pleases the Father.

The more you spend time in God's presence through worship, the more strength you'll gain to stand on the Word of God in the midst of the pressure you're facing. Before you know it, you will have worshiped your way right out from under the pressure. And you will have passed The Pressure Test.

DISCUSSION STARTERS

1. How do you normally deal with pressure (eating, smoking, crying, etc.)?

2. Which of the steps to passing The Pressure Test are you doing well? Which steps do you need more help performing?

3. What actions will you take to manage pressure more effectively? What tools will you need to do so?

Chapter Four

The DISTRACTION TEST

The purpose of The Distraction Test is to find out if you will recognize a demonic distraction for what it really is and remain steadfast in what God has told you to do, or if you will put the will of God on hold long enough to answer the door for the devil. If someone fails The Distraction Test by losing sight of his God-given assignment and focusing instead on the distraction, he will miss out on the miracle God is trying to work on his behalf.

IMAGINE A FAIRLY large man is blocking your way. He's in a fighting stance, and for some reason you have to get past him. Because of his size, it would be very challenging for you to just walk up, knock him down, and step over him. This guy is ready for action—he's focused, he's stable, he's balanced properly, and he's big. He has his eyes on you. He understands that you're the assignment right now. He's prepared for trouble, and the only thing he's paying attention to is you.

That man would be difficult to get past. But what if this same man is leaning casually against the wall with his feet crossed at the ankles? Let's say a lovely lady has come up beside him, and she's flirting, blowing kisses, and batting her eyelashes. He wouldn't seem so impossible to get past then, would he?

That's because he's distracted. He's not watching you closely now; in fact, he's so intent upon flexing his muscles to impress the young lady he may not be paying any attention to you at all. Not only has his focus wandered, but also his stance is so relaxed that if he had to change position suddenly, it would be difficult for him to keep his balance. I'd say this would be a good time for you to make your move.

Now imagine this same sort of scene in the spirit realm, only this time it's the devil that wants to get past you. You're the one on guard. The Bible says, "Be sober, be vigilant; because your adversary the devil, as a roaring lion, walketh about, seeking whom he may devour" (1 Pet. 5:8). The devil can't just devour anybody at any time, so he has to look for somebody who is distracted, has a visible weakness, or has left a door open so he can pounce on hm.

When we're on top of our game—when we're paying attention, we have our eye on the prize, and we're focused on what God has said—it's difficult for the enemy to push us out of the way or knock us down. When we are determined and focused and vigilant, the devil doesn't stand a chance—and we will successfully pass *The Distraction Test*.

The purpose of The Distraction Test is to find out if you will recognize a demonic distraction for what it really is and remain steadfast in what God has told you to do, or if you will put the will of God on hold long enough to answer the door for the devil. If someone fails The Distraction Test by losing sight of his God-given assignment and focusing instead on the distraction, he will miss out on the miracle God is trying to work on his behalf.

PETER IS TESTED

The Word of God is filled with examples of people who were given The Distraction Test. Let's take a look at what happened when God tested Peter.

> And straightway Jesus constrained his disciples to get into a ship, and to go before him unto the other side, while he sent the multitudes away. And when he had sent the multitudes away, he went up into a mountain apart to pray: and when the evening was come, he was there alone. But the ship was now in the midst of the sea, tossed with waves: for the wind was contrary. And in the fourth watch of the night Jesus went unto them, walking on the sea. And when the disciples saw him walking on the sea, they were troubled, saying, It is a spirit; and they cried out for fear.
>
> But straightway Jesus spake unto them, saying, Be of good cheer; it is I; be not afraid. And Peter answered him and said, Lord, if it be thou, bid me come unto thee on the water. And he said, Come. And when Peter was come down out of the ship, he walked on the water, to go to Jesus. But when he saw the wind boisterous, he was afraid; and beginning to sink, he cried, saying, Lord, save me. And immediately Jesus stretched forth his hand, and caught him, and said unto him, O thou

of little faith, wherefore didst thou doubt? And when
they were come into the ship, the wind ceased.

—Matthew 14:22–32

Peter is in the middle of a bona fide miracle! He's walking
on water! He has walked way out from the boat to where Jesus
was, but then he gets distracted. The distraction has nothing
to do with the miracle. What in the world do the wind and
the waves have to do with walking on the water? Is it easier to
walk on water when it's a calm, clear day?

Of course not! But in this case the purpose of the demonic
distraction is to get Peter's mind off what God has him doing
right now. Satan knows if he can get Peter's mind onto something else, Peter will lose out on the miracle.

The word *distract* means "to draw (the sight, mind, or
attention) in different directions; to perplex or confuse."[1]
Distractions come to hijack your faith so that it will stop
working on the blessing God set up for you. Distractions come
to turn your attention to something that has nothing to do
with what God said.

If you intend to ever pass The Distraction Test, you must
first learn how to recognize distractions. Distractions come in
all shapes, sizes, and colors. Relationships can be a distraction.
Doctor's reports can be a distraction. Even promotions can be
a distraction. Everything that appears to propel you forward is
not necessarily good for you. Every door that opens for you is
not always a good door. Some doors open as part of a test to
see if you'll take the bait and accept the opportunity instead of
doing what you know the Lord told you to do.

You must learn how to recognize the little demonic things

that show up in your life that have nothing to do with the will of God. You must understand that if you get distracted and spend time with something on the sidelines that has nothing to do with what God told you to do, it's going to cost you the miracle that's in front of you.

Passing The Distraction Test requires you to learn how to focus on God's plan when everything around you is chaotic. Begin by asking yourself, "What did God tell me to do?" Many times obeying God means saying, "I don't have time to stop and deal with what everybody else wants from me."

When you obey God, some people will call you "mean." Some will call you "cold." Others will say you're not walking in love because you won't stop to fix a problem they didn't take time to get your input on *before* they got into the mess. Learn how to stay focused on what God is saying to you right now. Not letting people draw on you and get you distracted is a huge part of passing The Distraction Test.

NEHEMIAH IS TESTED

It takes determination and focus to win in the fight of life. Nehemiah was living at a time when the children of Israel had gone into captivity and the wall around the city of Jerusalem had been knocked down. The wall was an important part of the people's defense, so Nehemiah accepted the assignment to go and rebuild the wall—and he miraculously completed this task in fifty-two days.

The Bible says, "Now it came to pass when Sanballat, and Tobiah, and Geshem the Arabian, and the rest of our enemies, heard that I had builded the wall, and that there was no breach left therein; (though at that time I had not set up the doors upon the gates;) that Sanballat and Geshem sent unto me, saying, Come, let us meet together in some one of the villages in the plain of Ono. But they thought to do me mischief" (Neh. 6:1–2).

Nehemiah is up on the wall doing his job. Then some enemies show up and want to work out a peace treaty. "Let's get together," they say. "Let's talk this thing out." Isn't it amazing that they weren't interested in a treaty until he began this assignment?

Nehemiah refused to let them distract him: "I sent messengers unto them, saying, I am doing a great work, so that I cannot come down: why should the work cease, whilst I leave it, and come down to you?" (Neh. 6:3).

Notice the mind-set Nehemiah had: "Why should I stop doing what God told me to do and put His program on pause to do something that has nothing to do with His will—even if it's for only two hours?" So far Nehemiah has passed The Distraction Test.

The enemy will try to pull you off your assignment. It doesn't matter to him what you are doing while you're off focus. All he cares about is that you're not doing what the Lord told you to do. His ultimate goal is to make you flunk the test.

In Nehemiah's story the enemy kept trying to get him off track. "They sent unto me four times after this sort; and I answered them after the same manner. Then sent Sanballat his servant unto me in like manner the fifth time with an open letter in his hand" (Neh. 6:4–5).

In those days they didn't have a postal service like we have in the United States today. You couldn't just stick a stamp on a letter and drop it in a box for delivery. In Nehemiah's day letters were carried by hand from one person to the other.

Typically they were flattened and sealed on both ends or rolled up and sealed with wax to make sure nobody else read the letter. A king or other important person would push the signet of his ring into the wax to make sure it was read only by the intended recipient. Some letters were delivered in a nice bag or with a ribbon tied in a bow.

The letter Sanballat sends to Nehemiah is an open letter. It's not in a bag. It's not flattened. It's not rolled up. Sending an open letter like that was a sign of contempt or disrespect. Because his simple request didn't get Nehemiah to stop working on the wall, Sanballat was apparently trying to use disrespect to make Nehemiah so angry he would come off the wall.

This is where many believers flunk The Distraction Test. We allow our emotions to upset us. We get involved in a little altercation. Someone hurts our feelings. We are passed over for a promotion. Instead of trusting the Lord to take care of things, we fall for these demonic distractions and try to deal with the situation on our own—and we usually make a bigger mess than we had before we started.

Nehemiah read Sanballat's open, disrespectful letter: "Wherein was written, It is reported among the heathen and Gashmu saith it, that thou and the Jews think to rebel: for which cause thou buildest the wall, but thou mayest be their king, according to these words. And thou hast also appointed prophets to preach of thee at Jerusalem, saying, There is a king in Judah: and now shall it be reported to the king according to these words. Come now therefore, and let us take counsel together" (Neh. 6:6–7).

Sanballat is basically saying, "I heard you want to be king. You're building this wall so you and your people can rebel. If you don't come down off this wall, I'm going to tell the Persian king on you." Sanballat is trying to distract Nehemiah by getting him to defend his name.

I love Nehemiah's response. "Then I sent unto him, saying, There are no such things done as thou sayest, but thou feignest them out of thine own heart" (Neh. 6:8).

Nehemiah said, "Nobody told you that. Boy, stop lying! You're just making stuff up." Nehemiah wasn't about to stop his assignment just to straighten out this little mess. Nehemiah wasn't about to let himself fail The Distraction Test. He was determined to accomplish what the Lord told him to do.

PETER IS TESTED...AGAIN

Shortly before Jesus was crucified, Peter betrayed Jesus three times by failing to acknowledge Him. After Jesus was raised from the dead, He sent a special message to Peter letting him know that despite his denial, he was still in good grace with the Lord.

> But go your way, tell his disciples *and Peter* that he goeth before you into Galilee: there shall ye see him, as he said unto you.
>
> —MARK 16:7, EMPHASIS ADDED

Jesus took the time to single Peter out to make sure Peter knew He was not angry with him and that he was still welcomed. Wow! What an awesome display of love Jesus showed. But here comes Peter's Distraction Test. Instead of going somewhere to pray, meditate, and seek the will of God for his life, Peter shifts into default mode. He goes fishing, which was his trade before he became one of Jesus's disciples.

Peter and the rest of the boys fished all night, and they caught nothing. Around sunrise Jesus showed up and yelled out to them, "Have you caught anything?"

Not recognizing Jesus, they said, "Nothing."

Then Jesus told them, "Put your net over to the right side of the boat and pull in a great catch." They followed His instruction and pulled in all these fish. And at that moment they recognized Jesus.

After they'd brought their catch in to shore, Jesus tried to get Peter back on track. Peter was fishing when he should have been preaching. He was distracted because he messed up, and he was focusing on his mistake instead of getting back on the path of righteousness.

Jesus addressed Peter's problem head-on. "So when they had dined, Jesus said to Simon Peter, Simon, son of Jonas, lovest thou me more than these? He saith unto him, Yea, Lord; thou knowest that I love thee. He saith unto him, Feed my lambs" (John 21:15). Jesus is saying to Peter: "Get focused on what I told you to do."

Jesus continued to challenge Peter. "He saith to him again the second time, Simon, son of Jonas, lovest thou me? He saith unto him, Yea, Lord; thou knowest that I love thee. He saith unto him, Feed my sheep" (John 21:16). Jesus is again telling Peter to get focused on what He told him to do.

But Jesus wasn't finished with Peter. "Simon, son of Jonas,

lovest thou me? Peter was grieved because he said unto him the third time, Lovest thou me? And he said unto him, Lord, thou knowest all things; thou knowest that I love thee. Jesus said unto him, Feed my sheep" (John 21:17). Notice that Jesus told Peter to get focused *three* times.

At this point Jesus reminds Peter of what he was supposed to be doing. "Verily, verily, I say unto thee, When thou wast young, thou girdest thyself, and walkedst whither thou wouldest: but when thou shalt be old, thou shalt stretch forth thy hands, and another shall gird thee, and carry thee whither thou wouldest not. This spake he, signifying by what death he should glorify God. And when he had spoken this, he saith unto him, Follow me" (John 21:18–19).

Jesus ends their conversation by essentially telling Peter, "It's OK now. Come on and follow Me." Now Peter is back on track with Jesus, and he is confident he will never be distracted again—at least for about a minute.

"Then Peter, turning about, seeth the disciple whom Jesus loved following; which also leaned on his breast at supper, and said, Lord, which is he that betrayeth thee? Peter seeing him saith to Jesus, Lord, and what shall this man do? Jesus saith unto him, If I will that he tarry till I come, what is that to thee? follow thou me" (John 21:20–22).

Before they had taken two steps, Peter was already worrying about what was going to happen in somebody else's life. For any of us The Distraction Test can come in the form of concerns about what's going on in somebody else's life. Someone else gets a new house, a new car, or a new spouse, so we begin to feel bad about our lives. But the Lord says the same thing to us that He said to Peter: "What does that have to do with you?"

AUDITING POTENTIAL DISTRACTIONS

The distractions Satan uses to get us off track can be subtle, but it is possible to pass this test. There are three basic keys to remember.

Keep your eyes on Jesus.

The Word of God tells us in Hebrews 12: "Therefore then, since we are surrounded by so great a cloud of witnesses [who have borne testimony to the Truth], let us strip off and throw aside every encumbrance (unnecessary weight) and that sin which so readily (deftly and cleverly) clings to and entangles us, and let us run with patient endurance and steady and active persistence the appointed course of the race that is set before us, Looking away [from all that will distract] to Jesus, Who is the Leader and the Source of our faith [giving the first incentive for our belief] and is also its Finisher [bringing it to maturity and perfection]. He, for the joy [of obtaining the prize] that was set before Him, endured the cross, despising and ignoring the shame, and is now seated at the right hand of the throne of God" (vv. 1–2, AMP).

We must look away from everything that will distract us. This means we have to take an audit of what's going on in our lives. We have to be honest: Is this relationship a distraction? Is the new job a distraction? Are my plans for the future a distraction? Everything that distracts you is not necessarily a sin, but the devil will use anything to take you off course. That is why you must guard yourself against anything that will get your mind off what God wants you to focus on right now.

Toughen up enough to keep your focus.

The Bible says, "Endure hardship with us like a good soldier of Christ Jesus. No one serving as a soldier gets involved in civilian affairs—he wants to please his commanding officer" (2 Tim. 2:3–4, NIV). We need to do what it takes to keep focused—and that requires some mental and emotional toughness.

There will always be things that try to pull you off course and keep you distracted. There always will be people who'll try to make you feel bad because you don't chase after every emergency that pops up on their radar screens. You can't let yourself be moved by people who get mad at you for obeying God.

That's a lesson I had to learn as a pastor. Someone is always coming in with an emergency, but I can't always make it *my* emergency. I simply cannot let myself get distracted by everyone who walks through the door saying, "I want to see only the pastor." I know sometimes they get mad when I can't counsel with them the moment they walk in, but if I let other people control my schedule, how could I show up at church with a fresh word from God to meet the needs of the congregation?

I was deeply touched by an incident I heard about that took place during World War II. There were two best friends, both fighter pilots, sitting in their planes on the runway with their engines running, in line to take off on another mission. When they received the go signal, they looked over at each other and gave each other a thumb's up.

After the first pilot took off, his engine stalled as he was climbing, and his plane went into a dive and exploded as it hits the ground. His best friend in the other plane witnessed the whole thing, and he was next in line to take off.

Later he admitted that his emotions were telling him to stop everything and say, "I can't do this now." But he was a first-class soldier. He recognized that there was nothing he could do for his friend. "If I don't take off now," he told himself, "countless people are going to lose their lives because I got distracted by something—even something as significant as my friend losing his life." This man passed The Distraction Test.

A number of years ago a well-known pastor was hosting a conference. On the night he was scheduled to speak, he received word that his niece had been killed in a tragic car accident.

He went to the hospital and made sure all of his family members who were involved in the accident were receiving proper care. But he didn't cancel the conference. Instead this minister went immediately from the hospital to the arena and preached his heart out. He didn't tell anyone what had happened until the meeting was over.

When asked why he responded this way, the pastor said God wasn't the one who killed his niece, so why should he let something the enemy did stop him from doing what God told him to do? This man passed The Distraction Test—and we can too if we will toughen up enough to stay focused and keep doing what God has instructed us to do, even in the midst of chaos.

Let God be God.

The Word says you should live your life "casting the whole of your care [all your anxieties, all your worries, all your concerns, once and for all] on Him, for He cares for you affectionately and cares about you watchfully" (1 Pet. 5:7, AMP).

You must be willing to trust God to work out the details surrounding whatever the distraction is while you're pursuing what He told you to do. The reason we end up coming down off our wall so many times (instead of staying put as Nehemiah did) is because we're trying to play God. We're trying to fix this person's problem over here. We're trying to solve that situation over there.

But if you're going to stay focused and remain distraction free, you have to let it all go and trust God with the details. He can do it so much better than you can anyway. He knows every detail about every person and everything involved in the matter. God wants to do His job, so release the reins and let Him be God.

DISCUSSION STARTERS

1. Which distractions arise most frequently in your life?

2. In what ways can relationships with family or friends create major distractions that hinder you from accomplishing what God has called you to do?

3. What action should you take, or what behaviors should you avoid, to keep from becoming a distraction in someone else's life?

Chapter Five

The LOT TEST

*The purpose of The Lot Test is to reveal whether you
are willing to completely remove yourself from the sins
of your past and never return to that life, or if you've
simply taken a temporary time-out since you accepted
Christ. The Lot Test will expose whether you have left
enough doors open in your life to get back to Egypt when
the excitement of being a new Christian wears off.*

IN COLLEGE I was the president of my fraternity at Michigan State University. I was the one hosting all the parties on campus. During football and basketball season my dorm room was the one everybody hung out in to watch the games. Occasionally, when there was a big boxing match on pay-per-view, I'd rent a room so we could all watch the fight together.

Then came the day when I decided to wholeheartedly give my life to God. My friends were OK with my newfound faith as long I was still doing all the stuff I used to do. But when I decided I was going to give my life completely to God, they didn't understand that. All of a sudden I'm no longer the life of the party. I'm not drinking anymore. I'm not going the same places and doing all the other things I used to do anymore. And just like that, the phone stopped ringing.

God created us human beings to be in fellowship and have companionship, so I enjoyed being with my college friends. But as much as I liked being a part of the action, I had to tell all of them I was never going to another party again—that I didn't even want to be invited. I knew I had to position myself so that I couldn't go to the next party even if I wanted to. I had to make an irrevocable decision of quality to go all the way with God.

This is something all believers need to learn how to do. From the day you get saved and start trying to walk uprightly before God, there is a constant tug that's trying to drag you back into the life of sin you came out of. This is the enemy trying to see if he can get you back into the lifestyle you left behind.

If you are not constantly on alert and keeping your defenses up, you may find yourself drifting back to the place of wickedness and sin. This is what happened to Abraham's nephew, Lot—which is why I call this *The Lot Test*.

The purpose of The Lot Test is to reveal whether you are willing to completely remove yourself from the sins of your past and never return to that life, or if you've simply taken a temporary time-out since you accepted Christ. The Lot Test will expose whether you have left enough doors open in your life to get back to Egypt when the excitement of being a new Christian wears off.

When Abraham took his nephew, Lot, with him when he left Ur of the Chaldees, a lot of problems arose. One problem was that the servants Lot brought with him were quarreling and fighting with Abraham's servants. The two men sat down to talk it over. "We do not want there to be any strife between us," Abraham said. "We're family. So you may choose any section of land you want, Lot, and whatever land you do not take, I'll take." So that's what they did.

> Abram dwelled in the land of Canaan, and Lot dwelled in the cities of the plain, and *pitched his tent toward Sodom.* But the men of Sodom were wicked and sinners before the LORD exceedingly.
> —GENESIS 13:12–13, EMPHASIS ADDED

This is how Lot ended up living in Sodom and Gomorrah. When Abraham, who was called Abram at the time, gave Lot the opportunity to choose which section of land he was going to take, not only did he choose the best land, but he also "pitched his tent toward Sodom."

Lot could see what was going on in Sodom from his home. He wasn't living there yet, but he was at least looking in that direction. He could hear what was going on. I'm sure passersby were telling him some of the "good" things about Sodom and Gomorrah. The location was also great for business. If Lot was selling cattle or crops harvested from his fields, he could take advantage of the economic benefit of being located right next to two major cities.

In other words, Lot justified his decision by saying, "Well, I know what they're doing is wrong, but I'm not doing it." He begins by *facing* Sodom and Gomorrah. Then he gets closer and closer to Sodom and Gomorrah until finally he winds up *in* Sodom and Gomorrah.

AN OPPORTUNITY TO ESCAPE

There was a time when some enemies captured Lot while he was in Sodom. And just as He does with us, God gave Lot an opportunity to escape the situation before real judgment began to fall. God used Abraham and his trained men to rescue Lot by force.

But as soon as Abraham got him out, Lot went right back to Sodom. (See Genesis 14:14–16.) Lot had grown attached to the city and found comfort in the midst of the wickedness. This often happens with people after they are delivered. They return to a life filled with darkness because it's familiar. As the Bible says, "They prove the point of the proverbs, 'A dog goes back to its own vomit' and 'A scrubbed-up pig heads for the mud'" (2 Pet. 2:22, THE MESSAGE).

When God decided it was time to destroy Sodom and Gomorrah for their wickedness, He sent two angels to help Lot move his family out of the area. When the angels arrived, they found Lot sitting at the gate of Sodom. He was now one of the public officials greeting people as they entered the city.

Later that evening, when a mob surrounded his house to have sex with his two angelic visitors, Lot went out to speak with them. "Brothers," he said—he is so deeply ingrained in this wicked place that he considers them his brothers—"I beg of you, do not behave so wickedly." Notice their reply:

> But they said, Stand back! And they said, This fellow came in *to live here temporarily*, and now he presumes

to be [our] judge! Now we will deal worse with you than with them.

—GENESIS 19:9, AMP, EMPHASIS ADDED

It's interesting to note that what began as Lot's temporary plan ended up having life-altering consequences. Why? *You cannot manage sin*!

UNMANAGEABLE

We have to reach the point where we become mature and honest enough to say, "There is something or somebody in my life that is slowing me down from reaching the goal God has ordained for my life." We can't sit around and play the "it's not hurting me" or "it's not bothering me" or "I can handle it" game because *sin cannot be managed.*

The reason you can't manage sin is because sin is never satisfied. If you give sin one small open door, your system will adjust to that level of sin and want more. Perhaps somebody sent you an e-mail, and when you open it, a pop-up appears. Curiosity gets the best of you, and you follow the bunny trail and mistakenly end up on a pornography website. Before you know it, you have an ungodly memory embedded in your system because of something inadvertently set before your eyes.

If you do not do something to safeguard your web browsing, you'll be back—same time, same channel—hoping for one more illicit glimpse. If you don't take some action to protect yourself, you'll tell yourself, "I'm going to do this only one more time." But one more time turns into two more times, then three, and so on until you have created a habit.

Once your system gets accustomed to viewing porn, it will start to scream at the thought of you stopping it. You can be saved for fifteen or twenty years and have been free from pornography (or whatever the issue of your past was), but the enemy will still poke and prod you to see if he can get you to go back to where you used to be. This basically is what happened to Lot and his family.

> And when the morning arose, then the angels hastened Lot, saying, Arise, take thy wife, and thy two daughters, which are here; lest thou be consumed in the iniquity of the city. And while he lingered, the men laid hold upon his hand, and upon the hand of his wife, and upon the hand of his two daughters; the LORD being merciful unto him: and they brought him forth, and set him without the city. And it came to pass, when they had brought them forth abroad, that he said, Escape for thy life; look not behind thee, neither stay thou in all the plain; escape to the mountain, lest thou be consumed. And Lot said unto them, Oh, not so, my LORD: Behold now, thy servant hath found grace in thy sight, and thou hast magnified thy mercy, which thou hast shewed unto me in saving my life; and I cannot escape to the mountain, lest some evil take me, and I die: Behold now, this city is near to flee unto, and it is a little one: Oh, let me escape thither, (is it not a little one?) and my soul shall live.
>
> —GENESIS 19:15–20

Despite the mercy of God, Lot still didn't voluntarily leave. The angels had to drag him and his family out of Sodom and Gomorrah. They tell him he needs to get far away and not look back. Lot says, "Fine, I'm going to leave. But just let me go right down the street."

Lot didn't want to get too far away. He was willing to leave, but he was hoping to return. "When all is said and done," he figured, "I can turn around and get back to business as usual." After they got away from the city, Lot's wife turned around because she just had to get one more glimpse of their home—and she turned to salt (Gen. 19:26).

How did Lot get so attached to Sodom and Gomorrah? It began when he caught a tantalizing glimpse of the place. It is so very important to be mindful of what you see. One of the ways good or bad enters your heart is through the "eye gates." What you constantly place before your eyes will indeed enter your heart and impact your perspective.

DON'T LOOK BACK

The devil doesn't care if you have been saved for two weeks, two years, or twenty years. He will constantly hang around, waiting for an opportunity to knock on your door and invite you to return to the place you used to be. This is The Lot Test. How many doors do you have cracked open in your life that could potentially take you back into bondage?

You have to constantly pay attention and watch for clues. Ask yourself, "Why am I reconnecting with this person from my past? Why am I thinking about these things? Why am I revisiting things I closed the door on years ago?"

The devil will use anybody and anything to get you to just look back. That's all he wants you to do initially—just take a look. Just pitch your tent in the direction of sin. Just take another peek at what it used to be like.

How do you avoid ever going back? *Don't look!* Get your eyes fixed on the prize that is out in front of you. And get so consumed with where God is trying to take you that you don't have time to consider where you used to be.

Do not leave any little doors cracked open. Do not leave yourself any room to return to what you used to do. If pornography is something you struggled with in the past, then put a code on your cable box. Get appropriate filters for your computer so you can't view porn sites. Tell your spouse what the issue has been.

Become accountable to somebody so you do not have this little secret nobody else knows about. As long as you're living with the secret, there's always a chance that on one of those days when you're not on top of things, the enemy will come knocking on your door.

This is what The Lot Test is all about. The devil is trying to see if he can get you to glance back as Lot's wife did. But you can't afford to go back. You can't afford to even look back. Instead you need to be determined that you're going to press forward and keep from opening your life and your family line to demonic attacks.

PROTECTING YOUR FAMILY LINE

Familiar spirits are demons that become familiar with a particular family for generations. They know the issues that have been that family's downfall. This is why you can look at many family lines and see a long string of alcoholism, infidelity, divorce, or teenage pregnancy. It's because there are demonic spirits that have been assigned to that particular family for the express purpose of keeping each generation bound.

When someone in the family gets saved, the enemy is not happy that the power he had over that family line has been broken. But if the individual doesn't guard his heart with the Word of God, the enemy will return to see if there's a way for him to oppress him again. Luke 11:24 says, "When the unclean spirit is gone out of a man, he walketh through dry places, seeking rest; and finding none, he saith, I will return unto my house whence I came out."

The word *house* here does not only mean a dwelling place, like the home we live in. It also means a family or generation. When a person in your family line gets saved, the demonic spirit that has tormented your family for years gets kicked out. The demon goes around seeking a new place to rest but can't find any, so he will come back. It may be two or three weeks later, or it may be two or three generations later. But he will come back.

"And when he cometh, he findeth it swept and garnished. Then goeth he, and taketh to him seven other spirits more wicked than himself; and they enter in, and dwell there: and the last state of that man is worse than the first" (Luke 11:25–26). If he comes back and finds the house empty, swept, and garnished, he'll say, "OK, I'm not coming by myself. I'm going to go and get seven spirits more wicked than I am." And when these demons arrive, they entrench themselves back into that family line.

How did that person end up worse off than before? He didn't have enough safeguards in place when the enemy came, so he failed The Lot Test.

You need to be aware of whatever you struggled with before you got saved, and you need to become familiar with what your parents and grandparents, and aunts and uncles, and everyone else in your family line has struggled with. Even if you're not dealing with those issues, you owe it to your children to put enough of the Word of God inside of them, and to plead the blood of Jesus over them, so that when familiar spirits come by to tempt your children, they will pass The Lot Test.

ENJOYING THE PROMISED LAND

"Brethren, I count not myself to have apprehended: but this one thing I do, forgetting those things which are behind, and reaching forth unto those things which are before, I press toward the mark for the prize of the high calling of God in Christ Jesus" (Phil. 3:13–14).

As I mentioned before, I enjoy being around people. If you knew me at all, you would know I'm a family- and friendship-oriented person. I'm the type who wants to include everybody and take everybody along for the ride.

But I learned years ago that if I tried to drag everybody along with me, none of us would get anywhere. I've discovered that there are some people who do not want to go to the Promised Land—or, more precisely, they do not want to do what it takes to go to the Promised Land. They want the benefits of the Promised Land, but they want them while still living in Egypt.

Sadly I've realized I can't bring all my friends with me. Through the years I have invited many of my friends to church. Some of them showed up once or twice, but they didn't make attending church part of their lifestyle. As a result they're still struggling with the same things we both used to struggle with, but today I'm free.

All we can do is give people an opportunity to be exposed to the same Word that has changed our lives. People have to decide for themselves that they want to go hard after everything God has for them. And there are some people you have to love from a distance until they determine they are willing to sell out to God as you have.

This doesn't mean you're better than they are or that you should stop praying for them. What it means is that you are making sure those individuals don't become a temptation for you to look back toward Sodom. It means you're willing to distance yourself from the temptation in order to safeguard your heart.

Jesus said, "Remember Lot's wife" (Luke 17:32). You may feel like holding the hand of someone who is content being in bondage and is not ready to leave. But if you do, that means you're either in bondage yourself or very close to it. If your friend or family member wants to stay in Egypt, then you're going to have to let go of his hand so you can enter the Promised Land.

There is too much at stake for you to allow the enemy to turn your heart back to the very things God delivered you from. Not only can you miss the will of God for your own life, but also your children and your children's children can be negatively affected as well. Don't give Satan the satisfaction! Keep your eyes on God and allow Him to move you to the next level as you pass The Lot Test.

DISCUSSION STARTERS

1. Did Lot pass or fail The Lot Test? Why?

2. Since God always gives us a way of escape from sin, why do we still sometimes flunk The Lot Test?

3. What familiar spirits have you noticed in your family line? What steps can you take to stop those spirits from continuing to oppress your family?

4. Have you ever discovered that you'd left a door open to sin? How did you, or will you, close that door?

Chapter Six

The TEST of BEING MISUNDERSTOOD

The purpose of The Test of Being Misunderstood is to discover if you are mature enough to live free from the opinion and acceptance of the crowd. This test will gauge whether God can trust you in times of great pressure to do what is right instead of bowing to what is popular. This is a test for leaders!

HAVE YOU EVER wondered how Moses was able to continue leading the children of Israel—and not get discouraged and quit—when time after time they misunderstood almost everything he said and did?

They watched as Moses delivered them from Pharaoh, rescued them from Egypt, and parted the Red Sea to bring them through on dry ground. Yet they accused him of leading them into the wilderness to make them die of starvation and thirst. They accused him of leading them out of Egypt to be slaughtered by giants. They talked about him because he married an Ethiopian woman—even his sister and brother disagreed with his decision to marry her!

The crowd was always talking about Moses, always misunderstanding his intentions, and always questioning his motivations. Yet the Bible says he was one of the most humble men to ever walk the face of the earth.

Leaders are always at risk of being misunderstood. The word *misunderstood* means "incorrectly understood or interpreted" or to be "unappreciated."[1] The purpose of *The Test of Being Misunderstood* is to discover if you are mature enough to live free from the opinion and acceptance of the crowd. This test will gauge whether God can trust you in times of great pressure to do what is right instead of bowing to what is popular. This is a test for leaders!

Leaders must learn how to pass The Test of Being Misunderstood—or else they'll always walk around with their feelings hurt, ready to quit or fight. And since those who usually misunderstand never keep it to themselves, leaders will feel the pressure to defend their name and set the record straight to everyone who could have the wrong idea about them. All of those things are one big waste of time!

The pressure from being misunderstood can cause you to turn your attention toward retaliating against the person who misunderstood you instead of remaining focused on God's will for your life. Don't take the bait! You have to realize that all of this is happening to uproot the Word of God from your heart and get you off track.

We read in Mark 4:16–17, "And these are they likewise which are sown on stony ground; who, when they have heard the word, immediately receive it with gladness; and have no root in themselves, and so endure but for a time: afterward, when affliction or persecution ariseth for the word's sake, immediately they are offended."

When the Word has been sown into the stony ground of our hearts and we receive it with gladness, we begin to grow and flourish. Satan can see we're on a path that will lead to our becoming stronger in God, so he tries to get us to release the Word we've received. The enemy brings about what I like to call the "squeezing season." This is when he unleashes a lot of pressure on you through two vehicles—affliction and persecution.

Affliction is pressure caused by circumstances. When you have a financial challenge, it brings pressure. When you get a bad doctor's report, it brings pressure. When you have confusion in your home, it brings pressure. These are all examples of afflictions.

Persecution, however, is pressure other people bring upon you. When the words or actions of people make you want to change your mind about a quality decision you've made, that's persecution.

The enemy uses this kind of pressure to get you to return to the nice, comfortable "religious" life you used to have instead of being sold out and totally committed to God. If you let that happen, you will simply blend into the crowd instead of standing out as the leader you were destined to be. If you're not able to handle people talking about you and misunderstanding your motivation for doing things, you will never be able to get promoted to a higher level in God.

HOW MOSES PASSED THE TEST

So let's look at the reason Moses matured to the place where he was no longer moved by those who misunderstood him. If you're familiar with the life of Moses, you'll know that he was born during a time when the reigning pharaoh in Egypt had disregarded the previous arrangement with Joseph and the children of Israel. Pharaoh also decided that the Israelites were multiplying too fast, so he gave instructions that all the newborn baby boys should be thrown into the river.

When baby Moses became too difficult to hide, his mother placed him inside a basket and put it in the Nile River in hopes of protecting him. Pharaoh's daughter saw the baby floating in the basket and took him into her home and raised Moses as her own son.

Now fast-forward to when Moses is about forty years old. Since he was raised with the Egyptians, he hasn't been a slave like the rest of the Hebrews. He hasn't been made to suffer the same hardships as his people, yet he knows he is a Hebrew. He wants to be accepted and have a sense of belonging.

One day Moses sees an Egyptian beating up a Hebrew, and when he thinks no one is looking, he kills the Egyptian and hides the body in the desert. The next day he's out among the Hebrews, and two Hebrew men are fighting. Moses tries to be a mediator—"Can't we all just get along?" But one of the Hebrews says, "Who gave you the right to tell us what to do? Are you going to kill us too?"

Now Moses realizes the secret is out, and soon everyone will know that he murdered the Egyptian. So he flees Egypt and spends the next forty years out in the wilderness alone with God.

It is during these forty years that Moses finally gets the revelation that the only opinion that really matters is God's. That's what qualified him to go back and deliver the children of Israel. He had grown to the point that he was able to ignore what Pharaoh had to say about him. He was able to ignore even what the Hebrews had to say about him. He cared only about what God said about him.

For the next forty years he led the children of Israel through a wilderness despite their bickering, arguing, and murmuring the whole time, and he didn't quit. Moses had passed The Test of Being Misunderstood. He just had to keep reminding himself, "I'm on a mission to do the will of God."

HOW ABRAHAM FLUNKED THE TEST

Just as the Bible gives us examples of how to do things well, it also give us examples of how *not* to do things. Abraham's story is a good example of how not to take The Test of Being Misunderstood. God gave Abraham instructions to leave all of his kindred behind and go to the land God would show him. Abraham left his home, but he didn't leave everyone behind— he brought his nephew, Lot, with him.

Personally I believe Abraham took Lot because Lot's dad— who was Abraham's brother—had died. I also believe Abraham didn't want to have to deal with his other relatives misunderstanding him and saying, "How could you abandon your only nephew when he was counting on you?"

But if you're going to get bumped up to another level of leadership in the kingdom of God, you have to be able and willing to deal with people misunderstanding you, even if those people are your family. As long as you know in your heart that what you are doing is right before God, let that be enough.

Sometimes your family is not going to understand you. Sometimes friends are not going to understand you. Sometimes the people in your church are not going to understand you. Once you have made up your mind to obey God, you can't run around and take a vote to see what everyone thinks about it.

HOW JESUS HANDLED BEING MISUNDERSTOOD

The Bible says Jesus was tempted in all the ways we are, and He certainly knew how it felt to be misunderstood. We see a prime example in the Gospel of Matthew when Jesus was brought before the Jewish council.

> Now the chief priests, and elders, and all the council, sought false witness against Jesus, to put him to death; but found none: yea, though many false witnesses came, yet found they none. At the last came two false witnesses, and said, This fellow said, I am able to destroy the temple of God, and to build it in three days. And the high priest arose, and said unto him, Answerest thou nothing? what is it which these witness against thee? But Jesus held his peace, and the high priest answered and said unto him, I adjure thee by the living God, that thou tell us whether thou be the Christ, the Son of God. Jesus saith unto him, Thou hast said: nevertheless I say unto you, Hereafter shall ye see the Son of man sitting on the right hand

of power, and coming in the clouds of heaven. Then the high priest rent his clothes, saying, He hath spoken blasphemy; what further need have we of witnesses? behold, now ye have heard his blasphemy. What think ye? They answered and said, He is guilty of death. Then did they spit in his face, and buffeted him; and others smote him with the palms of their hands, Saying, Prophesy unto us, thou Christ, Who is he that smote thee?

—MATTHEW 26:59–68

Why is Jesus going through all of this? Because He has been misunderstood. He was talking about his body when He said, "You destroy this temple, and in three days I'll raise it up again." But they found a couple of guys off the street who were willing to testify against Him: "We heard Him say He can knock down the temple, and He'll build it back up in three days."

This would have been a perfect opportunity for Jesus to say, "That's not what I meant!" Though Jesus could have spoken up and explained Himself, the Bible says He held His peace. Why did He remain silent? Jesus knew He was doing what was pleasing to God, and that's all that mattered. His accusers' opinion of Him didn't count. So Jesus felt it was better to make sure He stayed right with the Father than to allow these people to bait Him into an argument that was going to pull Him off His course.

Jesus was often misunderstood—by the crowds, by the Jewish religious leaders, by the Roman authorities—but on one occasion it was His own followers who misunderstood Him.

> Then Jesus said unto them, Verily, verily, I say unto you, Except ye eat the flesh of the Son of man, and drink his blood, ye have no life in you. Whoso eateth my flesh, and drinketh my blood, hath eternal life; and I will raise him up at the last day. For my flesh is meat indeed, and my blood is drink indeed. He that eateth my flesh, and drinketh my blood, dwelleth in me, and I in him....Many therefore of his disciples, when they had heard this, said, This is an hard saying; who can hear it? When Jesus knew in himself that his disciples murmured at it, he said unto them, Doth this offend you?...From that time many of his disciples went back, and walked no more with him. Then said Jesus unto the twelve, Will ye also go away? Then Simon Peter answered him, Lord, to whom shall we go? thou hast the words of eternal life.
>
> —JOHN 6:53–68

This time Jesus's own disciples were the ones who misunderstood Him. Jesus said to them, "You're going to have to eat My flesh and drink My blood." Even though most of these people had been with Him for three years and He had never said anything like that before, no one raised his hand and asked, "Can You explain what You mean?" No one gave Him the benefit of the doubt by saying, "I'm sure He didn't really mean it that way."

Instead, they said, "This is a hard saying. Who can listen to this kind of preaching?" And many of them walked away.

Notice that Jesus didn't run after them, begging them, "Please don't leave My church!" He let them go and turned to the twelve disciples and said, "What about you guys? Are you going too?"

Jesus wasn't willing to even clarify His statement to a bunch of carnal believers who would have known what He was talking about if they'd spent enough time in prayer. Or, if they didn't understand what He meant, at least they could have trusted that He had a purpose for making that statement after having seen His impeccable character for so many years.

By asking, "Will you go away too," Jesus was basically saying, "If you don't know what I'm talking about, and you don't love and trust Me enough to believe I'm not trying to hurt you, then you probably should go ahead and leave." He was interested only in doing God's will, and He was not concerned about being misunderstood. You must have the same mentality if you're going to accomplish the great work God has for you to do.

KEYS TO PASSING THE TEST OF BEING MISUNDERSTOOD

If what you've been reading challenges you or bears witness in your spirit, it's because God is trying to get you in a position to be used in a greater capacity in the kingdom of God. He's asking you the central question of The Test of Being Misunderstood: "Are you going to stay behind, nurse your wounds, and worry about what people think of you? Or are you going to just do what God has told you to do?" If you want to pass this test, there are three keys to keep in mind.

1. Don't allow another human being to determine your self-worth.

Consider Jesus's example. John 2:23–25 says, "Now when he was in Jerusalem at the passover, in the feast day, many believed in his name, when they saw the miracles which he did. But Jesus did not commit himself unto them, because he knew all men, and needed not that any should testify of man: for he knew what was in man."

The Bible says Jesus wouldn't commit *Himself* to the people, even though they were cheering Him on and talking about what an anointed preacher He was and how many miracles He had performed. Obviously, He loved the people. He was willing to give His life for them and to forgive them as He was dying on the cross. But He didn't let what they thought of Him affect His self-worth. Jesus didn't allow His self-image to depend upon everybody else's opinion of Him.

Are you letting someone else determine your self-worth? Has someone else's voice become the barometer in your life that decides whether you're doing a good job? The only person who owns that right is God Almighty. Yes, of course we submit to government leaders. Yes, we thank God for employers. Yes, we honor those who have been put in spiritual authority in our lives. But at the end of the day, there's only one person whom we need to hear say, "Well done!" If you're receiving applause from everyone around you but heaven has nothing to say, none of that praise matters!

2. Keep your eyes on your own business.

We read in 1 Thessalonians 4:9–11, "But as touching brotherly love ye need not that I write unto you: for ye yourselves are taught of God to love one another. And indeed ye do it toward all the brethren which are in all Macedonia: but we beseech you, brethren, that ye increase more and more; and that ye study to be quiet, and to do your own business, and to work with your own hands, as we commanded you."

Some of us get ourselves into trouble because we entangle ourselves in other people's affairs. When you don't mind your own business, you can often end up being misunderstood. If it doesn't concern you, keep your mouth shut. Just pray for the people involved. If they ask you what you think about the issue, *then* share your wisdom with them. But if they never ask your opinion, keep it to yourself. This will keep you from being misunderstood, and it will prevent you from being caught up in unnecessary drama. Just tend to what you have going on in your own life.

3. Live a righteous life that speaks for itself.

The Word of God says, "[And see to it that] your conscience is entirely clear (unimpaired), so that, when you are falsely accused as evildoers, those who threaten you abusively and revile your right behavior in Christ may come to be ashamed [of slandering your good lives]" (1 Pet. 3:16, AMP). The Message Bible says it this way: "Keep a clear conscience before God so that when people throw mud at you, none of it will stick. They'll end up realizing that they're the ones who need a bath."

In other words, people can talk about you. They can misunderstand you. They can throw mud at you. But if you live right long enough, the mud won't stick. Your good name will be cleared up—not because you were fighting to make it right, but because you did right long enough for people to know your true character.

When you do these three simple things, you will not get sidetracked from your life's mission. You will be able to pass The Test of Being Misunderstood, and God will see that He can trust you to be the leader He desires and needs you to be.

DISCUSSION STARTERS

1. How do you know if you're passing The Test of Being Misunderstood?

2. Can you recall a time when you felt pressure from being misunderstood? What did the pressure make you want to do?

3. Do you find it easier to pass The Test of Being Misunderstood at certain times more than others? Why?

4. Is there anything significant in your past (an absentee parent, rejection, etc.) that would leave you vulnerable to failing this particular test?

Chapter Seven

The CONFRONTATION TEST

The purpose of The Confrontation Test is to see how long it will take for you to learn to handle conflict and confrontation in a manner that is pleasing to your heavenly Father instead of defaulting to infantile measures. This test determines whether you are ready for mature benefits in the kingdom or if you still need to be nurtured as a babe. It is the elevator button that indicates your ability to lead others and determines how high you're allowed to go.

WHEN MY SIBLINGS and I were young, there was one thing my mother simply would not stand for. If I came home and told her I got into a fight with some guy at school because he tried to jump on my little brother, I'd be OK—even if I was suspended from school for it.

But if I came home and got into a fight with my brother—if

I had the audacity to fight against my own flesh and blood—that was a completely different thing! It didn't matter why we were fighting. She didn't want to hear my side of the story. She didn't want to hear his side of it. The fighting stopped right then and punishment ensued.

I understand what that was all about now. And if your parents were like my mom, I bet you do too. As parents we don't want to see our kids fighting each other. It's bad enough to hear them squabbling, but when their quarrels turn into punches thrown, it strikes a parent to the core. I love my children with all my heart. But there's one thing that will cause me to correct them in a hurry—and that's when I see them fighting each other.

How do you think God feels when He sees His children fighting? As God sees it, we're members of the same family. We should be supporting one another. When God does something in our brother's or our sister's life, He wants us to be excited about it! Our heavenly Father wants us to look for ways to help our brothers and sisters in Christ go to the next level instead of fighting one another.

The last thing God wants is for those who are benefiting the most from His power to cause one another pain and create division in His body. That's why we need to pass *The Confrontation Test*.

The purpose of The Confrontation Test is to see how long it will take for you to learn to handle conflict and confrontation in a manner that is pleasing to your heavenly Father instead of defaulting to infantile measures. This test determines whether you are ready for mature benefits in the kingdom or if you still need to be nurtured as a babe. It is the elevator button that indicates your ability to lead others and determines how high you're allowed to go.

As with any of the tests we face, you don't have to pass The Confrontation Test to go to heaven. God loves you just as you are. As long as you have received Jesus as your Lord and Savior, you will spend eternity in the presence of God. But if you want the benefits and blessings that come from being mature in your relationship with God, you'll need to pass these tests.

"Think of it this way. If a father dies and leaves an inheritance for his young children, those children are not much better off than slaves until they grow up, even though they actually own everything their father had" (Gal. 4:1, NLT). We're not ready to receive our inheritance—all the blessings Jesus died on the cross to give us—until we grow up.

Even when we're babies, we are bona fide members of the family. Legally speaking, even though we're very young, our full inheritance belongs to us. But that doesn't mean we get the keys to the car until we're mature enough to drive. If we want to grow up and receive our full inheritance, we must learn how to successfully pass The Confrontation Test.

If you are in leadership—in the church, the marketplace, or the family—or if you occasionally find yourself thrust into positions of leadership, this is one of those tests you'll take repeatedly. The details will be different, the players will be different, but the way we pass The Confrontation Test will be the same every single time.

THE REAL TEST OF MATURITY

Paul begins his first letter to the Corinthian church by affirming that these believers are doing some things right.

> I thank my God always on your behalf, for the grace of
> God which is given you by Jesus Christ; that in every
> thing ye are enriched by him, in all utterance, and in
> all knowledge; even as the testimony of Christ was
> confirmed in you: So that ye come behind in no gift;
> waiting for the coming of our Lord Jesus Christ: Who
> shall also confirm you unto the end, that ye may be
> blameless in the day of our Lord Jesus Christ.
>
> —1 Corinthians 1:4–8

Paul is telling them, "It's clear that you're growing in the
Word and you're operating in the gifts of the Spirit." But after
he praises them, he admonishes them: "Now I beseech you,
brethren, by the name of our Lord Jesus Christ, that ye all
speak the same thing, and that there be no divisions among
you; but that ye be perfectly joined together in the same mind
and in the same judgment" (1 Cor. 1:10).

Obviously something was stirring in the church at Corinth.
Although this congregation had some qualities that made
them seem mature in the things of God, evidently strife and
division were still getting the best of them. In other words,
they were acting immaturely—and they were failing The
Confrontation Test. This is even clearer in Paul's admonition
in 1 Corinthians 3.

> However, brethren, I could not talk to you as to spiri-
> tual [men], but as to nonspiritual [men of the flesh,
> in whom the carnal nature predominates], as to mere
> infants [in the new life] in Christ [unable to talk yet!]
> I fed you with milk, not solid food, for you were not
> yet strong enough [to be ready for it]; but even yet you

are not strong enough [to be ready for it], for you are still [unspiritual, having the nature] of the flesh [under the control of ordinary impulses]. For as long as [there are] envying and jealousy and wrangling and factions among you, are you not unspiritual and of the flesh, behaving yourselves after a human standard and like mere (unchanged) men?

—1 Corinthians 3:1–3, AMP

Was the apostle Paul expecting the Corinthian believers to act like something other than mere human beings? Of course he was! The Corinthians had been born again. That means they were transformed on the inside. Paul was expecting them to allow the new nature of the Spirit of God to dominate the nature of the flesh. This means they would handle conflicts in a way that was completely different from how they handled them before they were saved.

The Bible says we have "the mind of Christ" (1 Cor. 2:16). But the mind of Christ is one that is constantly being renewed as we read and meditate on the Word of God. So the task of every Christian is to let the Word renew his way of thinking until he has evicted his old mind-set.

But if there's ever a time when the old way of thinking will try to come back, it's when we're in the midst of a confrontation. You have to be armed and ready at all times. The Confrontation Test is not one of those tests that you get ten weeks to study for—it's a pop quiz!

You wake up one morning to the sound of birds singing, and you're happy as a lark. You feel the blessings of God raining down on you. Then before you know it—*POW!*—you're face-to-face with a brother or a sister who "has something to say to you." All of a sudden it's time to take The Confrontation Test. If you haven't been saturating in the Word and renewing your mind, your old way of thinking will rise to the surface, and you'll find yourself responding in a manner that you never intended.

Like the Corinthians, you can know the Word of God and have the gifts of the Spirit operating in your life but still fail The Confrontation Test. The real test of your spiritual maturity is how you handle conflict and confrontation.

Paul said, "For this was my purpose in writing you, to test your attitude and see if you would stand the test, whether you are obedient and altogether agreeable [to following my orders] in everything. If you forgive anyone anything, I too forgive that one; and what I have forgiven, if I have forgiven anything, has been for your sakes in the presence [and with the approval] of Christ (the Messiah), to keep Satan from getting the advantage over us; for we are not ignorant of his wiles and intentions" (2 Cor. 2:9–11, AMP).

When you choose to forgive and walk in love, you are demonstrating that you're not ignorant of Satan's devices. Satan's job is to find out if you're a genuine thoroughbred Christian—or just a knockoff. In this passage Paul is asking the Corinthians: "Are you going to forgive or not?" He wants to know if they are going to pass The Confrontation Test.

HOW TO HANDLE CONFRONTATION

How did Jesus instruct us to behave in the midst of confrontation? He said, "If your brother wrongs you, go and show him his fault, between you and him privately. If he listens to you, you have won back your brother" (Matt. 18:15, AMP).

Some people think the godly way to handle confrontation is not to deal with it at all, but this is not the case. It's not good enough to sit idly on the sideline. You can't just ignore a conflict and let people do whatever they want. Jesus isn't telling you to just sit there and be a punching bag.

He said if your brother offends you, go to him and tell him his fault or the issue you have with him. This should be a conversation between you and your brother *alone*. The moment you go and start telling everybody else how upset you are with this person, know that you have just flunked The Confrontation Test.

If you feel you need some wisdom to make sure you're approaching things the right way, go to somebody who is mature enough to counsel you according to the Word of God. Don't go to some hot-headed friend who's going to jump in and make matters even worse. If the real reason you're going to talk with someone is to vent and "get things off your chest," don't expect God to give you a passing grade and promote you.

If the person won't hear you when the two of you discuss the issue, the next step is to get other people involved. The Bible says, "But if he does not listen, take along with you one or two others, so that every word may be confirmed and upheld by the testimony of two or three witnesses" (Matt. 18:16, AMP).

Notice the reason you're bringing other people into it—*"so that every word may be confirmed."* You're not taking people who are on your side so you can gang up on the other person and prove you're right and he's wrong. You're simply inviting two or three people to come along and be unbiased witnesses.

Naturally you will want to choose these people wisely. If you bring your sister and your best friend, it may be hard for them to be impartial.

And, of course, if you bring a group of supporters when you show up to talk with the other person, what do you think will go through the other party's mind? "Oh, no you didn't! Did you bring all of your friends so you can team up on me?" He's automatically going to be defensive no matter what you say if all the people with you are on your side.

So when you take two or three witnesses with you, take people who don't have a stake in the matter, who don't have their emotions involved, and who are mature enough to listen to both sides and not support only you. God's purpose for having you bring others with you is so someone else can hear what each party said and nothing can be misconstrued later.

Remember, the two people in the confrontation have so many emotions running through them they will probably miss some of what's really being said. God's will is that someone with good sense and a clear head would come and help the two parties sort things out.

What happens if even that doesn't work? "If he pays no attention to them [refusing to listen and obey], tell it to the church; and if he refuses to listen even to the church, let him be to you as a pagan and a tax collector" (Matt. 18:17, AMP). If there's still no resolution to the problem after you've taken two or three witnesses with you, take the situation to those who have spiritual authority over you.

Talk with one of the pastors or ministers at your church and let him sit down with the two of you and help you work things out. At this point, if the other person involved will not listen even to the pastor, you should pray for him, but you won't be able to have fellowship with him.

I've observed that when believers are mature enough to go to the person directly and talk things over, it often turns out that the confrontation is just a misunderstanding. When you begin by going to the person—without bringing a whole bunch of other people into it, or without them hearing about it from three or four other sources who have nothing to do with the situation—you can often fix the problem before it becomes a big issue. But if you find that the issues still cannot be resolved between the two of you, follow the progression outlined in the Bible.

CONFRONTING FAILURE

Unfortunately many Christians don't handle confrontation in the way Jesus taught us. For the most part it's not because they haven't heard this before. My experience is that there are four reasons Christians fail to handle conflict according to the Word.

The first reason involves their *emotions*. When you are emotionally charged, you're not thinking clearly, and your emotions are dictating what's going to take place. Emotions cause us to default to our pre-Christ way of handling conflict. When people respond to conflict emotionally, they typically react in one of four unhealthy ways: they *fight, fake, fold,* or *flee.*

We know what it means to *fight.* That's when you go toe-to-toe with the person. "I'm going to tell you what I think and give you a piece of my mind!"

To *fake* is to sit back and act like nothing is bothering you. "Nothing is wrong with me. I'm always this way." This happens a lot with Christians who attend churches where the Word of God is really being taught. They want to act like they're so mature and spiritually strong that things don't bother them. But instead of being phony, it's better to just be honest and stop acting like nothing is wrong.

Another unhealthy way people respond emotionally to conflict is to *fold*. To fold means you just give in every time. It's to say, "I don't want to deal with the conflict. I'd rather do it your way." That's not healthy either.

Eventually these people will get frustrated with living a life they didn't plan on living because they kept giving in to what everyone else wanted whenever conflict arose. No one likes confrontation, but if you're ever going to be promoted in God, you have to learn how to disagree in a way that brings glory to God.

The last unhealthy way people emotionally handle conflict is to *flee*. They take off and run. They think, "I need a time out! I need a break from this!" So they resign from the department, leave the church, quit their job, or divorce their husband or wife. The only problem is that no matter where they run, the problem is still there—and often it has gotten worse.

While some people respond emotionally to conflict, other Christians fail to handle confrontation the way Jesus taught because *they love drama*. They enjoy getting the attention that comes with having problems.

If they handled things God's way, no one would be calling, e-mailing, and texting them about what's going on in their life. They would rather talk about the situation with someone— often someone who is spiritually immature—than get rid of the problem. Having drama in their life gives them a rush!

The third reason Christians handle confrontation improperly is because of *fear.* They're afraid of the one-on-one encounter. They're afraid of having to actually talk with the other person in a mature way and express how they feel. They may have plenty of courage when they're in a group but simply can't handle one-on-one interaction.

Even if the person you have an issue with is someone you are submitted to, if he is a mature leader, he's not going to be offended by the fact that you came to talk with them—as long as you're doing so in a respectful way.

The last reason Christians don't deal with conflict the way Jesus instructed stems from *hurt and rejection.* Often people who have been hurt and rejected many times react to a current conflict out of their past hurt. They automatically get defensive as things that happened to them in the past begin to replay in their minds like a movie. But if they are going to grow up enough to pass The Confrontation Test, they will have to recognize that every person they deal with is not a replica of the one who hurt them before.

PASSING WITH FLYING COLORS

Once we make a quality decision to handle all conflict in a God-honoring manner, there are four keys that will help us pass The Confrontation Test with flying colors.

Humility

The Bible says, "Brethren, if a man be overtaken in a fault, ye which are spiritual, restore such an one in the spirit of meekness; considering thyself, lest thou also be tempted. Bear ye one another's burdens, and so fulfil the law of Christ" (Gal. 6:1–2).

Before you speak to the other person, first consider your own failings and shortcomings in order to keep a proper perspective. Otherwise you may approach the conflict from a position of superiority or self-righteousness. Just stop for a minute and say, "Have I messed up anything before? Have I ever said something that was offensive to someone? I don't want to go to this person from a superior position, so let me humble myself because I realize I've messed up before too."

Even if the person who offended you seemed to have had wrong motives and intended to hurt you, there is probably somebody out there who has felt you did something intentionally to hurt them as well. Recognize that you're going to get better results if you go to the person with a humble attitude than if you go with a sense of self-righteousness.

Love

First Corinthians 13:8 tells us that "love never fails" (NKJV). If you want to pass The Confrontation Test, you must be sure you're operating in love. If you don't love the person, then you're not ready to confront him. You need to take time to pray for the individual first. It's amazing what happens when you pray for someone. God will soften your heart and allow you to go to the other person with the right intent. Having stirred up a godly love for the person you're confronting, you will desire God's will for him instead of your own.

Patience

James 1:4 says, "But let patience have her perfect work, that ye may be perfect and entire, wanting nothing." Patience allows us to exercise proper restraint and hear the other person out. Impatience is a manifestation of anger and intolerance. It has no place in conflict resolution. You must be patient when you go to resolve a conflict. Patience will allow you to listen to the other person's entire story. There may be something in what he or she is saying that you haven't considered.

Containment

Proverbs 26:20 says, "For lack of wood the fire goes out, and where there is no whisperer, contention ceases" (AMP). You have to keep your conflict from spreading to others. In other words, you must contain it. Let your issue be your issue. Don't poison the minds of others about another person.

You're bigger than that. Don't try to get all of your friends to dislike a person. Always keep in mind that this problem didn't involve them. Like a firefighter clearing a perimeter around a fire that has potential to spread, you must keep a space around yourself and not allow your issue to spread to others. Instead, put the fire out. Do what you can to protect others from getting hurt. Be mature enough to put water, not gasoline, on the flames.

YOU CAN DO IT!

The Confrontation Test is about more than just our relationship with other people—it goes to the very heart of our relationship with God. Consider Paul's words to the Ephesians.

> I therefore, the prisoner of the Lord, beseech you that
> ye walk worthy of the vocation wherewith ye are called,
> with all lowliness and meekness, with longsuffering,

forbearing one another in love; endeavouring to keep
the unity of the Spirit in the bond of peace.
—Ephesians 4:1–3

When someone comes against us, our human tendency is
to react the moment we are offended: "You make me mad, so
now I'm going to straighten you out!" But God expects us to
respond to confrontation the way Jesus did.

Has anybody spit on you? Have they ridiculed you? Have
they ripped the beard from your face? Have they taken a crown
of thorns and crushed it into your skull? Have they mocked
you, laughed at you, stripped you, and hung you up naked in
front of a crowd that watched you bleeding to death?

We walk in a worthy manner when we are walking like
Jesus—in humility and long-suffering. It's never time to start
telling someone how offended you are if you haven't been exer-
cising some long-suffering. Romans 14:19 says, "So let us then
definitely aim for and eagerly pursue what makes for harmony
and for mutual upbuilding (edification and development) of
one another" (amp).

If you have been handling conflict or confrontation in a
way that is not according to the Word of God, take time right
now to ask the Lord to forgive you. Make the decision to never
flunk The Confrontation Test again.

Do what you can to live peaceably with everybody. When
there is conflict or confusion, look for a way to work it out.
Don't allow yourself to get angry with those who oppose you.
When someone is speaking against you or mistreating you,
your heavenly Father is waiting for you to act as Jesus would.

God knows you can do it. He's like a loving father, sitting

in the grandstands of heaven, shouting to you: "You can do it! Just do what I taught you! You know what we've been practicing! Just do it!" Listen to the voice of your Father today. He's setting before you life and death, blessing and cursing. Choose life! Pass The Confrontation Test and let the world know you are mature enough to handle the higher place God wants to take you.

DISCUSSION STARTERS

1. Why does your potential for leadership depend upon your passing The Confrontation Test?

2. What do you think "longsuffering" (Eph. 4:1–3) might look like in the midst of confrontation?

3. Which of the four reasons Christians fail to handle confrontation properly have you been guilty of committing? What actions are you willing to take to make sure you don't repeat the same mistakes?

Chapter Eight

The MONEY TEST

The purpose of The Money Test is to determine what percentage of your heart you will trust and worship God with. This test is the entrance, midterm, and final exam of your spiritual maturity.

THERE IS A direct connection between money and the human heart. "Wherever your treasure is," Jesus said, "there the desires of your heart will also be" (Luke 12:34, NLT). The attitude we have toward our money reveals the truth about us, and that's why it is so important that we pass *The Money Test.*

The purpose of The Money Test is to determine what percentage of your heart you will trust and worship God with. This test is the entrance, midterm, and final exam of your spiritual maturity.

God doesn't require you to totally give up material things

or give away everything you own. But He wants you to have a healthy relationship with money and material possessions so you can be used by Him to be a blessing to others—by doing whatever He tells you, whenever He tells you, and for whomever He tells you.

If you have a wrong relationship with money, God will require you to release what you have—one way or another. He will allow you to encounter circumstances that will prove to you that material possessions can't come close to sustaining you. He wants you to know for certain that money makes a poor "god."

Money can't buy good health. Some of the richest people in the world have died from incurable diseases. They may have been able to afford the best doctors, and their influence may have been enough to get them bumped to the top of a transplant list, but their money couldn't make them well.

Money can't buy peace in the home. Every year magazines such as *Forbes*, *Time*, and *Fortune* list the richest people in the world. Some of these people have twenty billion dollars, but when you read the articles, most of the individuals admit to having been divorced two or three times. They have money, but they don't have peace. They keep switching mates, but they're looking for something they can get only from God.

WHO IS YOUR SOURCE?

We are constantly given opportunities to take The Money Test. When we develop a wrong relationship with money, God will allow opportunities to arise that show us we have been choosing money as our god.

Most people mess up on The Money Test when they begin

to focus on the money itself—how much they're giving to support the church or another ministry—instead of the bigger picture, which is whether they have truly surrendered everything to God, including their financial decisions. They don't understand that God is not concerned about the money—He's concerned about the heart.

Once when Jesus was teaching about money, He told a story about a man who had accumulated a lot of riches and goods but ended up flunking The Money Test.

> The ground of a certain rich man brought forth plentifully: and he thought within himself, saying, What shall I do, because I have no room where to bestow my fruits? And he said, This will I do: I will pull down my barns, and build greater; and there will I bestow all my fruits and my goods. And I will say to my soul, Soul, thou hast much goods laid up for many years; take thine ease, eat, drink, and be merry. But God said unto him, Thou fool, this night thy soul shall be required of thee: then whose shall those things be, which thou hast provided?
>
> —LUKE 12:16–20

Our hearts should never become consumed with material things. If they do, God will help us see that our material possessions could never truly replace Him.

What place does money have in your heart? Is money first place or is God? Most people will quickly say God is first because we all know that's the right answer. But the reality is, first place belongs to whomever or whatever you give most of your time and attention. First place is determined by what you do when you're forced to choose whether to trust God and do what His Word says or to handle your problems yourself.

Remember, wherever your treasure is, which is also going to be what you give first place to, is where your heart is going to be. If the treasure you're seeking is more stuff—having a bigger house, a bigger car, more material possessions—then that's where your heart is. Your heart cannot be wrapped up in God and material things at the same time.

Jesus said it this way: "Lay not up for yourselves treasures upon earth, where moth and rust doth corrupt, and where thieves break through and steal: But lay up for yourselves treasures in heaven, where neither moth nor rust doth corrupt, and where thieves do not break through nor steal: For where your treasure is, there will your heart be also. The light of the body is the eye: if therefore thine eye be single, thy whole body shall be full of light. But if thine eye be evil, thy whole body shall be full of darkness. If therefore the light that is in thee be darkness, how great is that darkness! No man can serve two masters: for either he will hate the one, and love the other; or else he will hold to the one, and despise the other. Ye cannot serve God and mammon" (Matt. 6:19–24).

Mammon means *money.* You cannot serve God and money. You can *have* both, but you can't *serve* both. God has to be number one in your heart.

What kind of relationship do you have with this material world and its possessions? Will you allow the fact that you don't have what you think you should have stop you from doing what God wants you to do? When the Lord speaks to your heart and tells you to give something to someone, will you stop for a minute to evaluate whether you can "afford" to obey Him?

The decisions you make in those moments—to do what your mind is telling you or to follow God's instructions—immediately determines who or what you are allowing to be your resting place and your security. God cannot and will not share the throne of your heart with anything or anybody else.

The only way to correct an unhealthy relationship with money is to learn that God alone is your source.

AN UNHEALTHY RELATIONSHIP

What would you do if all the money you had stored up in banks suddenly disappeared? It has been confirmed that terrorists have bombs that can use electromagnetic pulse (EMP) to knock out all the electronics within a certain radius. If such a bomb were to be detonated in your city, every electronic device in its path would be totally wiped out.

All of your bank's records would be gone. Showing the teller your checkbook or your receipts wouldn't do any good because they wouldn't be able to access your account information to verify it. At that moment you'd have to trust God.

It is crucial that your mind and heart are settled on the fact that money is not the reason you're successful. You must know beyond the shadow of a doubt that you are prosperous because you serve a God who will provide, no matter the need. Despite what happens in this world's economy, God will make sure you are still well taken care of.

The Bible gives us a good example of someone with an unhealthy relationship with money and material wealth in Jesus's encounter with the rich young ruler.

> And when he was gone forth into the way, there came one running, and kneeled to him, and asked him, Good Master, what shall I do that I may inherit eternal life? And Jesus said unto him, Why callest thou me good? there is none good but one, that is, God. Thou knowest the commandments, Do not commit adultery, Do not kill, Do not steal, Do not bear false witness, Defraud not, Honour thy father and mother. And he answered and said unto him, Master, all these have I observed from my youth. Then Jesus beholding him loved him, and said unto him, One thing thou lackest: go thy way, sell whatsoever thou hast, and give to the poor, and thou shalt have treasure in heaven: and come, take up the cross, and follow me. And he was sad at that saying, and went away grieved: for he had great possessions.
>
> —MARK 10:17–22

Obviously the rich young ruler had an improper relationship with money. On the outside this guy seemed to be spiritual and was doing a whole lot of things right. But in his heart money was taking center stage. He needed to pass The Money Test in order to turn things around.

When Jesus told the rich young ruler, "one thing thou lackest," He wasn't saying this man was perfect in every area of his life but there was one thing he needed to work on. What He was actually saying to him was: "You know the commandments—don't defraud, honor your father and your mother, do good to those around you, etc.—but there is still one commandment that you're lacking."

What's so shocking is that the one thing he was lacking—the

one commandment that the young man had *not* gotten right—is the very *first* commandment: "Thou shalt have no other gods before me" (Exod. 20:3).

When Jesus told the rich young ruler to sell what he had, he became sad. This is what happens so often at offering time in church. When people hear that it's time to receive the offering, they are "sad at that saying" because their hearts trust their money and not God to meet their needs.

How would you like to be that man and have Jesus assess your life and say you have only one shortcoming? Would you be willing to make that one thing right so you could be promoted in the things of God?

Jesus always used practical examples in His teachings. In Mark 10 Jesus tells His disciples what it would take for a rich man to enter the kingdom of heaven.

> And Jesus looked round about, and saith unto his disciples, How hardly shall they that have riches enter into the kingdom of God! And the disciples were astonished at his words. But Jesus answereth again, and saith unto them, Children, how hard is it for them that trust in riches to enter into the kingdom of God! It is easier for a camel to go through the eye of a needle, than for a rich man to enter into the kingdom of God. And they were astonished out of measure, saying among themselves, Who then can be saved?
> —MARK 10:23–26

Jesus was not saying that a rich person could not enter into relationship with God. He was making the point that a rich man cannot have a genuine relationship with God if he's still in love with his money. It's as we read earlier in Matthew 6:24: you cannot serve both God and money. Again, you can have both, but you cannot serve both. Jesus was indicating that if you don't have a proper relationship with money, it will quickly try to assume the role of mini-god in your life.

Many people have said, "God doesn't want us to have money because money is evil." Money is neither evil nor good. It is neutral. Money is simply a magnifier. If a person has an evil heart, money will simply afford him an opportunity to perpetuate evil on a grander scale. However, if a person has a benevolent heart, money will give him a platform for far more good than he would have been able to accomplish with little to no resources. So The Money Test really exposes the condition of your heart.

One thing many people don't realize is that God is not trying to take anything from you. He just wants to make sure that what you have does not become lord over you. Ultimately He wants your heart, not what's in your bank account. You will never give Him more than He will give you.

Jesus said, "Verily I say unto you, There is no man that hath left house, or brethren, or sisters, or father, or mother, or wife, or children, or lands, for my sake, and the gospel's, but he shall receive an hundredfold now in this time, houses, and brethren, and sisters, and mothers, and children, and lands, with persecutions; and in the world to come eternal life" (Mark 10:29–30).

You don't have to wait until you get to heaven to receive the blessings of God. Jesus said, "*Now*, in this time, God will restore your land, houses, and wealth. *Then*, in the world to come, you'll have eternal life." You won't need all of these earthly riches when you're walking around heaven. The streets are paved with gold there. He's going to give it to you while you're still here on the earth, where you can use it for His glory and honor. However, this will happen only when you demonstrate a right heart and a right relationship toward money.

GETTING BACK ON COURSE

When you don't know what God's Word says about a matter, you err and find yourself way off course. Jesus said, "You are in error because you do not know the Scriptures or the power of God" (Matt. 22:29, NIV).

A lot of times people make the wrong choices concerning money because they don't know what the Word of God says about it. They've never been taught how they should relate to God and their money. As a result, they are reluctant to put God first in the area of finances.

This might shock you, but I believe if you cannot give to God through your tithes and offerings with the right heart, then you should just keep it. You would do better to keep your money and just continue to meditate on the Word. Eventually God's going to be able to get in there and rearrange your way of thinking and change your heart.

When your heart is open to God, the error is going to go away. You will eventually get to a place where you know what the Scriptures say, and that will cause you to submit and honor God. When this happens, you will find out that God can take care of you so much better than you can take care of yourself.

A lot of people have the wrong information about money because they've been listening to the enemy's thoughts on the subject. They're struggling to pass The Money Test because they've been getting their answers from the devil's cheat sheet—and everything he says is a lie.

When I was in high school, every senior had to take economics and government in order to graduate. Most of us decided to take those classes in the summer and get them out of the way so we could have a shorter schedule in the fall. Once when we were taking an exam in our government class, one girl decided she wasn't going to study. She had a cheat sheet—a tiny piece of paper with a ton of answers written in very small print on the front and back. The rest of us had studied our little hearts out, and she sat there sliding her paper over to look at the answers, then sliding it back again.

Before long, the teacher called this girl's name and said, "What are you doing?"

The girl said, "Nothing."

The teacher said, "What is under your test?"

The girl said, "Nothing."

Then the teacher got up and walked over to the girl. We were all thinking, "It's on now!"

The teacher lifted up her test. There was the cheat sheet, and the girl was caught! The teacher took the cheat sheet back to her desk and started looking at it. Then she said, "If you were going to cheat, at least have the right answers on your cheat sheet!"

That's what happens with a lot of believers. They try to cheat God's system by thinking, "I can get ahead financially by doing things the way the world does them." They end up reading the devil's cheat sheet, and it always has the wrong answers on it.

Here's one wrong answer people listen to: "You're responsible for taking care of your own needs." You won't find God telling you that anywhere in His Word. The only time we are left to our own devices is when we get off God's program and start listening to the lies of the devil.

God wants to give us a carefree life like that of the birds and flowers:

> Therefore I say unto you, Take no thought for your life, what ye shall eat, or what ye shall drink; nor yet for your body, what ye shall put on. Is not the life more than meat, and the body than raiment? Behold the fowls of the air: for they sow not, neither do they reap, nor gather into barns; yet your heavenly Father feedeth them. Are ye not much better than they? Which of you by taking thought can add one cubit unto his stature? And why take ye thought for raiment? Consider the lilies of the field, how they grow; they toil not, neither do they spin: And yet I say unto you, That even Solomon in all his glory was not arrayed like one of these. Wherefore, if God so clothe the grass of the field, which to day is, and to morrow is cast into the oven, shall he not much more clothe you, O ye of little faith? Therefore take no thought, saying, What shall we eat? or, What shall we drink? or, Wherewithal shall we be clothed? (For after all these things do the Gentiles seek:) for your heavenly Father knoweth that ye have need of all these things. But seek ye first the kingdom of God, and his righteousness; and all these things shall be added unto you.
>
> —MATTHEW 6:25–33

You should not be worried about where your provision will come from tomorrow or if you're going to have enough to take care of your needs today. God is not urging you to be irresponsible, but He is saying you shouldn't let yourself walk around with cares weighing you down. When you walk around worried and fretful, you have taken on responsibility that isn't yours.

Where did we get the thinking that we have to take care of our own needs? We bought the lie from the devil's cheat sheet. Throughout Scripture God tells His people that if they honor Him with their wealth, He will always make sure all their needs are met and they have enough to be a blessing to someone else. That's called *overflow*!

LEARNING FROM EGYPT

No one knows what is going on in your heart except you and God. The Lord loves you enough to tell you what is needful in order for you to pass The Money Test, just as He told the rich young ruler, but it is up to you to decide. All God wants is for you to honor Him with your substance.

The principle is the same whether you have a little or a lot. Don't trust in what you have—trust in the God who gave you what you have. The Israelites had to learn this lesson the hard way. Just before the Israelites left Egypt, God told them they weren't going to leave empty-handed because they were His people.

He said, "And I will give this people favour in the sight of the Egyptians: and it shall come to pass, that, when ye go, ye shall not go empty. But every woman shall borrow of her neighbour, and of her that sojourneth in her house, jewels of silver, and jewels of gold, and raiment: and ye shall put them upon your sons, and upon your daughters; and ye shall spoil the Egyptians" (Exod. 3:21–22).

As the Israelites left Egypt, God loaded them up with money and jewels to fulfill the promise He made to Abraham. (See Genesis 15.) However, if we don't know what money is designed to do, we will treat it the wrong way, just as the children of Israel did.

> And when the people saw that Moses delayed to come down out of the mount, the people gathered themselves together unto Aaron, and said unto him, Up, make us gods, which shall go before us; for as for this Moses, the man that brought us up out of the land of Egypt, we wot not what is become of him. And Aaron said unto them, Break off the golden earrings, which are in the ears of your wives, of your sons, and of your daughters, and bring them unto me. And all the people brake off the golden earrings which were in their ears, and brought them unto Aaron. And he received them at their hand, and fashioned it with a graving tool, after he had made it a molten calf: and they said, These be thy gods, O Israel, which brought thee up out of the land of Egypt. And when Aaron saw it, he built an altar before it; and Aaron made proclamation, and said, To morrow is a feast to the LORD. And they rose up early on the morrow, and offered burnt offerings, and brought peace offerings; and the people sat down to eat and to drink, and rose up to play. And the LORD said unto Moses, Go, get thee down; for thy people, which thou broughtest out of the land of Egypt, have

corrupted themselves: They have turned aside quickly out of the way which I commanded them: they have made them a molten calf, and have worshipped it, and have sacrificed thereunto, and said, These be thy gods, O Israel, which have brought thee up out of the land of Egypt.

—EXODUS 32:1–8

Because the children of Israel had been subject to the Egyptians' ways for four hundred years, they didn't know how to have a proper relationship with the treasures God had given them. The Egyptians worshiped all types of gods because they believed these idols were the reason they prospered. When the Israelites decided Moses was taking too long talking with God on the mountain, they turned back to what they had seen in Egypt.

They said, "Let's make a god out of this stuff. It was good enough for the Egyptians, so it should be good enough for us." Moses had to plead their case to stop God from punishing them for their dishonor.

It's no different today. When we run up against a tough situation, it's easy to turn around and do what we've seen others do to get ahead. You know what the Bible says about tithing, but you say, "I have to take care of my own needs and my own house. I've got to do what I've got to do." From then on it becomes easy to think your hard work, education, and personal efforts have made you a "success." Without realizing it, you've just made a molten calf out of money. You may go to church on Sunday, but the god you really worship is at First National Bank!

You must kick that golden calf over and decide that Jehovah God is the Most High God. He cannot bless you as He wants to until you make a change.

PASSING THE MONEY TEST

When are you going to realize that if your job shuts down, God will still be God? The reason people get so panicked when they start hearing talks of layoffs is because they've made their job an idol. We ought to have the same attitude as the three Hebrew boys facing the fiery furnace—"Go ahead and do what you have to. The God in whom I trust is well able to deliver me." (See Daniel 3:1–30.)

Likewise we should be able to say, "God is well able to deliver me from the unemployment line. He's well able to deliver me from going hungry. The God I serve is well able to provide whatever I need!"

In order to pass The Money Test, you must give God credit for everything in your life. You wouldn't have the mind to get that education if it hadn't been for God. You wouldn't have the strength to get up and go to work if it weren't for God. You wouldn't be safe and protected long enough to gain wealth if it hadn't been for God. Everything we have is because of Him, and it all belongs to Him.

Keep in mind that this test is not about whether you give tithes or offerings—it's way bigger than that. There are people who give tithes and offerings every week and are still flunking The Money Test.

The Money Test is not: "Do I give it?" The Money Test is: "Do I give it and trust God?" Someone who gives and panics every time a financial hurdle shows up is failing the test. God wants to give you far more than you have right now. But He needs you to have the right relationship with the things He gives you. The Bible warns us against forgetting about God when we have obtained a certain level of wealth.

> Beware that thou forget not the LORD thy God, in not keeping his commandments, and his judgments, and his statutes, which I command thee this day: Lest when thou hast eaten and art full, and hast built goodly houses, and dwelt therein; and when thy herds and thy flocks multiply, and thy silver and thy gold is multiplied, and all that thou hast is multiplied; then thine heart be lifted up, and thou forget the LORD thy God, which brought thee forth out of the land of Egypt, from the house of bondage; who led thee through that great and terrible wilderness, wherein were fiery serpents, and scorpions, and drought, where there was no water; who brought thee forth water out of the rock of flint; who fed thee in the wilderness with manna, which thy fathers knew not, that he might humble thee, and that he might prove thee, to do thee good at thy latter end; and thou say in thine heart, My power and the might of mine hand hath gotten me this wealth. But thou shalt remember the LORD thy God: for it is he that giveth thee power to get wealth, that he may establish his covenant which he sware unto thy fathers, as it is this day.
> —DEUTERONOMY 8:11–18

When God has done everything He promised to do, that's not the time for you to grab the wheel and take over. He wants you to just climb into the backseat, go to sleep, and enjoy the ride. God wants you to trust Him and let Him drive you to that wealthy place so you have enough to minister to those He places on your heart.

Take the time to search yourself right now. If you see where you may not have fully trusted God in the area of finances, make a choice today to change. Tell God that you're making a decision to pass The Money Test.

Tell Him you will no longer trust in your money, nor will you continue to be afraid of running out. Instead you will trust in the Lord. Surrender everything you have to Him—including your income. If you've been missing the mark, simply repent. He is not angry with you. He loves you, and He wants to get you in a position where you will pass The Money Test.

DISCUSSION STARTERS

1. Why do you think so many Christians struggle to fully trust God with their finances?

2. What fears have you had to fend off in order to trust God with a full 10 percent of your earnings?

3. What adjustments do you need to make to pass The Money Test?

Chapter Nine

The DISAPPOINTMENT TEST

The purpose of The Disappointment Test is to determine whether you'll allow setbacks, cancellations, delays, and disappointments to break your will to press forward. It is designed to see if you will demonstrate enough Holy Ghost buoyancy to believe again and let the devil know that with Jesus Christ on your side you cannot be stopped and you will not quit. This test separates the "bulldogs" from the "kittens" and will determine how much of your inheritance you'll actually see.

WHETHER YOU KNOW it or not, you've been taking The Disappointment Test your entire life. In school perhaps you were picked last to be on the kickball team, *and disappointment set in.* Or maybe you received poor grades, *and disappointment set in.* Or maybe you found yourself without a date for the homecoming dance, *and disappointment set in.*

Perhaps you spent four or five years in college, gaining a great education, but found that there was no job waiting for you after graduation, *and disappointment set in.* Maybe you stood up in a church and pledged "till death do us part, for better or for worse," and for some reason the person you married chose to leave and not fulfill the promise you made to each other, *and disappointment set in.*

We all face The Disappointment Test at different times and at different levels of severity throughout our lives. The devil wants this test to crush your spirit and break your will to win. He wants to see if disappointment will make you quit. But God wants you to know that you don't have to give up. Even in the midst of your disappointment, He *will* bring you some good breaks that turn things around in your life!

The purpose of The Disappointment Test is to determine whether you'll allow setbacks, cancellations, delays, and disappointments to break your will to press forward. It is designed to see if you will demonstrate enough Holy Ghost buoyancy to believe again and let the devil know that with Jesus Christ on your side you cannot be stopped and you will not quit. This test separates the "bulldogs" from the "kittens" and will determine how much of your inheritance you'll actually see.

There are a lot of people who have given up hope that life will ever get better for them. Even though they're still getting up every day and going about their day-to-day business—going to work, taking care of their families, attending church, etc.—they don't have any real hope or a positive expectation that things are going to improve.

Disappointment kicks in when things we thought were

going to work out a certain way didn't work out that way. There are four primary sources of disappointment.

The first source of disappointment is *people* who let us down. Typically it's not strangers or those we barely know who disappoint us. Usually it is people we know well—people we care about—who let us down.

The psalmist talked about this kind of disappointment. "For it is not an enemy who reproaches and taunts me—then I might bear it; nor is it one who has hated me who insolently vaults himself against me—then I might hide from him. But it was you, a man my equal, my companion and my familiar friend" (Ps. 55:12–13, AMP). Disappointment hurts us so much more and cuts so much deeper when it comes from someone we expected to be on our side or someone we were counting on.

The second source of disappointment is *circumstances.* An unexpected bill arrives in the mail. A doctor's report is negative. A job or promotion doesn't come through. Some plans don't work out. These are all circumstances that can arise out of nowhere and take the wind out of our sails.

The third source of disappointment is much closer to home. It's when we let *ourselves* down. It hurts your heart when you had every intention of doing something the right way and miss the bull's-eye. You feel a lot like Peter, who promised Jesus, "If I have to die with you, I will never deny you." Then before the night was over—not even twenty verses later—he denied Jesus three times. Peter was so disappointed in himself that "he went out and he wept bitterly." (See Luke 22:61–62.) Likewise we can disappoint ourselves when we don't live up to the goal we have set in our hearts.

The fourth source of disappointment is when we think

God has let us down—at least that's how it feels. We know, of course, that God never really lets us down. No matter how we feel and no matter what the circumstance looks like, whenever it seems God hasn't come through, there's something we don't understand about the situation. God loves us too much and He's too true to His Word to ever let us down.

YOU SHALL RECOVER ALL

David experienced some disappointment in his life, and it led to a devastating situation and more disappointment.

> And it came to pass, when David and his men were come to Ziklag on the third day, that the Amalekites had invaded the south, and Ziklag, and smitten Ziklag, and burned it with fire; and had taken the women captives, that were therein: they slew not any, either great or small, but carried them away, and went on their way. So David and his men came to the city, and, behold, it was burned with fire; and their wives, and their sons, and their daughters, were taken captives. Then David and the people that were with him lifted up their voice and wept, until they had no more power to weep. And David's two wives were taken captives, Ahinoam the Jezreelitess, and Abigail the wife of Nabal the Carmelite. And David was greatly distressed; for the people spake of stoning him, because the soul of all the people was grieved, every man for his sons and for his daughters.
>
> —1 SAMUEL 30:1–6

David and his army returned to their camp and found it had been burned to the ground, and all their wives and children had been taken captive. This was an overwhelming loss for these tough, battle-hardened soldiers. The Bible says the men "wept, until they had no more power to weep."

What David knew that the rest of the men didn't know was that the whole reason they left their families to go fight was because David had allowed the disappointment from his relationship with King Saul to get the best of him. You'll recall that as a young boy David was used by God to kill Goliath. Nobody else had enough courage to go out and fight the giant, but David knew he had a covenant with God and that the Lord would see him through the battle.

So David went out and killed Goliath. When he returned to the city with King Saul, the women in the street were dancing and singing David's praises. This made Saul so jealous of David that he wanted to kill him. King Saul recognized that David had an anointing on his life and might one day take away his throne, and he began looking for an opportunity to kill David.

Every so often an evil spirit would come upon King Saul and he'd become demented. When this happened, David would be summoned because when he played his harp for Saul, the evil spirit would lift off him. But after David left, the evil spirit would return, and King Saul's desire to murder David would increase.

When David finally learned that King Saul intended to kill him, he packed up and went on the run. He was running for his life, and King Saul was in hot pursuit. Once or twice during the time King Saul was chasing him, David had an opportunity to kill him. But instead of killing King Saul, David graciously spared his life. David honored the anointing on King Saul's life and was upright toward him at all times. On several occasions King Saul apologized to David, but he later turned around and wanted to kill him again.

David eventually got fed up with it. He was so disappointed with his relationship with Saul, who had been like a father figure to him, that David broke away completely—and even attempted to join the Philistine army.

The Philistines were the enemies of Israel. Goliath had been part of the Philistine army. But David was so disappointed with his relationship with King Saul that he was willing to fight with the Philistines against the Israelites.

While David was on the run, he had gathered an army of his own, and he took all of these soldiers with him to join the Philistines. But on the way to their first battle with the Philistine army, some of the Philistine generals spotted David and his men.

"Why in the world," they said, "would we let that Hebrew come with us? He may get us out there in the battle, and turn around and cut off all of our heads and deliver them to the Israelites to show them he's still on their side." (See 1 Samuel 29.) So David didn't go to battle against King Saul's army because the Philistine generals wouldn't let him join them.

Disappointed, the men went back home—and this is when they discovered their whole camp had been destroyed and their women and children had been kidnapped. They never would have been in this situation if David had not let his initial disappointment move him to do something he knew he had no business doing. He knew better than to fight against the Israelites. He knew the blessing of God was on the children of Israel, and he would never be able to overcome it.

David shouldn't have been out there with the Philistine

army, but the emotions stemming from that initial disappointment stirred him to take action. That's what disappointment does—it seeks to get you in an emotional place that makes you do something rash: "Go ahead and call it off!" "Go ahead and file for divorce!" "Go ahead and quit your job!" "Go ahead and curse that person out!"

The goal of disappointment is to get you to make a decision without consulting God. David failed The Disappointment Test in Ziklag. He had tried to fight off disappointment after disappointment, but they were unrelenting and finally made his heart sick. So he messed up and tried to join the Philistines.

Being outside the will of God, David left his household exposed. When he went back home, the camp was gone and all the women and children had been taken captive—and he's disappointed again. That's the way the enemy will try to defeat you. When you're still trying to recover from one series of disappointments, he'll try to hit you with another one.

DAVID RETAKES THE DISAPPOINTMENT TEST

When David arrived at his camp and saw that all the women and children had been kidnapped, this time he had enough sense not to let his disappointment move him. The enemy hoped he would allow his emotions to make him want to take his own life. Disappointment was saying, "Your spiritual father, Saul, doesn't love you anymore. Your wives and children have been taken captive. They may not even be alive. Everything you own has been burned to the ground. Your men are blaming you for this disaster. Go ahead and just end it right now. This situation is so bad, just go ahead and kill yourself. Take your life right now!"

But David had enough sense to know it wasn't time to leave. He knew that as long as God was still on his side, God could take this messed-up, terrible situation and make something good come out of it. The Bible says in the midst of his disappointment, "David encouraged himself in the LORD his God" (1 Sam. 30:6). David recognized that as long as God had not forsaken him, he still had a chance to win.

You may not always be able to get a friend or church member on the phone to encourage you. But you can always get in the mirror like David did and encourage yourself in the Lord. Tell *yourself* it will be all right.

When disappointment strikes and your emotions are going haywire, you have to learn how to tell yourself, "I know this thing is going to turn around. Despite what it looks like, God is still good to me. There is still room for a sudden move of God. There is still time for a sudden turn of goodness to come my way. I am still a child of the Most High God. I am still on the winning side. I am still the very righteousness of God in Christ Jesus. I still have the anointing of God working for me. I am not afraid that this won't work out for me. I believe God!"

Learn how to encourage yourself. Don't sit around and allow yourself to have a pity party. Don't withdraw from everyone. When disappointment strikes, the devil will try to make you think nobody cares about you. He understands that as long as you stay around people who will encourage you, it's going to be hard for him to take you out.

But if he can get you to believe the lie that nobody cares about you—not your family, not your friends, not the people at church—then you'll stay away from the very people who might encourage you. The enemy will also try to keep you from going to church, because if you show up at a service, you might be reminded that God is good all the time!

David realized that his emotions had gotten the best of him. David said, "I will not make the same mistake a second time. I will not let my emotions talk me into doing something crazy and messing up what God is trying to do."

When you're disappointed, don't ever make any major life decisions. Don't decide to end a relationship while you're disappointed. Don't decide to move to another city while you're disappointed. Don't decide to change churches or to stop serving while you're disappointed. Don't let yourself make any significant decisions when you're in the emotional upheaval of disappointment.

Get through the feelings of disappointment first; then you will be able to turn around and see the situation clearly. And you'll be able to hear the Spirit of God tell you what you ought to do about it. Making a decision in the middle of disappointment could compound the situation and make matters far worse.

Notice what David did after he encouraged himself in the Lord. "And David said to Abiathar the priest, Ahimelech's son, I pray thee, bring me hither the ephod. And Abiathar brought thither the ephod to David. And David enquired at the LORD, saying, Shall I pursue after this troop? shall I overtake them? And he answered him, Pursue: for thou shalt surely overtake them, and without fail recover all" (1 Sam. 30:6–8).

When David finally got his act together and his emotions in check, he went to God and said, "Lord, should I go after my stuff?"

God said, "Yes."

"Now, God," David said. "I don't want to go after it if I'm not going to get it. Will I get my stuff back?"

"Absolutely," God said. "You'll get it all back."

That's what God always says when you're trying to turn things around. If you ever ask God, "Am I going to win?" He'll say, "Yes!"

If you ask, "Am I going to get everything the enemy stole from me?" He'll say, "Absolutely! You'll get it all back."

God is not in the business of setting you up for failure. But you do have to get over any disappointment you feel so you can hear Him telling you it's going to be all right. If the only voice you are hearing is disappointment, then you won't hear what God has to say about your situation.

DISAPPOINTMENT IS UNAVOIDABLE

Even though no one else may understand, Jesus has been there. The Bible says our High Priest understands what we are going through when we are facing disappointment.

> Seeing then that we have a great high priest, that is passed into the heavens, Jesus the Son of God, let us hold fast our profession. For we have not an high priest which cannot be touched with the feeling of our infirmities; but was in all points tempted like as we are, yet without sin. Let us therefore come boldly unto the throne of grace, that we may obtain mercy, and find grace to help in time of need.
>
> —HEBREWS 4:14–16

Consider the disappointments Jesus faced. One of the people on His team, His treasurer, turned Him in to be crucified.

One of the guys in His inner circle, a man who was with Him everywhere He went and saw Him perform mighty miracles, pretended not to know who He was three times. His own countrymen screamed, "Set the murderer free! Put Jesus on that cross and crucify Him!" His own family came to interrupt one of His meetings, because they determined that He was "out of His mind" (Mark 3:21, NIV).

Jesus experienced disappointment at a level we will never understand, but to some extent we will all be disappointed. It's not an issue of *whether* you will face The Disappointment Test. You *will* go through things that leave you disappointed. There is no way to escape or prevent the disappointments that will come your way.

You don't have to live very long before you discover there are things in life you cannot control. But you can *always* control how you respond to them. The Bible says, "Rejoice not against me, O mine enemy: when I fall, I shall arise; when I sit in darkness, the LORD shall be a light unto me" (Micah 7:8).

One thing we can control is how much power we give the enemy. Our attitude should be, "Don't laugh at me so quickly, Mr. Devil. I may be down now—but when I fall, I shall arise. I don't care how many disappointments come my way. I am getting back up, and you'd better believe I'm getting back up every time!"

HOW TO OVERCOME DISAPPOINTMENT

It doesn't matter what disappointing circumstances come our way; there are two things you can do that are guaranteed to get you out of disappointment. The first thing you can do to pass The Disappointment Test is to *remember what the Lord has already done for you.*

> I waited patiently for the LORD; and he inclined unto me, and heard my cry. He brought me up also out of an horrible pit, out of the miry clay, and set my feet upon a rock, and established my goings. And he hath put a new song in my mouth, even praise unto our God: many shall see it, and fear, and shall trust in the LORD. Blessed is that man that maketh the LORD his trust, and respecteth not the proud, nor such as turn aside to lies. Many, O LORD my God, are thy wonderful works which thou has done, and thy thoughts which are to us-ward: they cannot be reckoned up in order unto thee: if I would declare and speak of them, they are more than can be numbered.
>
> —PSALM 40:1–5

The psalmist is saying that if he were to sit back and start trying to count up how good God has been to him, he'd never run out of things to say. The word *declare* in Psalm 40:5 comes from a Hebrew word that means "to announce, to rehearse, to report."

No matter what disappointment may come your way, you will pass The Disappointment Test if you do what your grandmother or grandfather may have told you: "Count your blessings, one by one. Count your blessings and see what the Lord has done." He woke you up this morning. He started you on your way. He has given you strength in your body, clothes on your back, and food in your stomach. He has given you the blood of Jesus Christ to save you from your sins.

When you start thinking about how good God has been to you, any disappointment you may feel will begin to seem insignificant. When disappointment comes, you just need to sit back and start counting your blessings. Start thinking about how good God has been to you.

The second thing you should do is *look for God to miraculously turn things around for you.* The Message Bible says, "Unrelenting disappointment leaves you heartsick, but a sudden good break can turn life around" (Prov. 13:12). Do you believe God can bring a sudden good break your way today?

I believe God has a sudden good break with your name on it. It may look like your situation is going in the wrong direction, like everything is falling apart, like things aren't going to work out the way you planned, like disappointment will get the best of you. But when God gives you a good break, everything will turn around for you—suddenly!

Believe God to do something suddenly for you that will turn your disappointment around. Don't allow the situation you're facing to cause you to tuck your tail and quit. Encourage yourself in the Lord, allow Him to order your steps, and let Him see you through to victory!

DISCUSSION STARTERS

1. Which of the four sources of disappointment tend to affect you the most? Why do you think this is so?

2. Can you think of a time when you failed The Disappointment Test—when your feelings of disappointment may have hindered or blocked God's will for your life? What happened?

3. What can you learn from past failures of The Disappointment Test? What can you do in the future to pass the test the next time you take it?

Chapter Ten

The OFFENSE TEST

This test will reveal whether you will allow offense to derail you from following the will of God. The Offense Test always comes to interrupt an impending spiritual promotion, and it is the test people fail most often. To pass this test, you must learn to submit to the Holy Spirit's leading instead of yielding to your emotions.

HOW WOULD YOU feel if you learned that your best friend was talking about you all around town? How would you feel if the owner of the company where you work suddenly hired his niece and asked you to train her to become your boss? How would you feel if, just when you were ready to move your relationship to the next level, you received a text message from your boyfriend or girlfriend calling it quits— "It's not you; it's me"?

What are these scenarios? They are opportunities to take

The Offense Test. This test will reveal whether you will allow offense to derail you from following the will of God. The Offense Test always comes to interrupt an impending spiritual promotion, and it is the test people fail most often. To pass this test, you must learn to submit to the Holy Spirit's leading instead of yielding to your emotions.

From a prison cell, Paul writes these words to the church in the town of Philippi: "And this I pray, that your love may abound yet more and more in knowledge and in all judgment; that ye may approve things that are excellent; that ye may be sincere and without offence till the day of Christ" (Phil. 1:9–10). Paul's prayer is that these believers will learn to cling to the things that are excellent and live without offense until the day Jesus Christ returns. I believe more people need to make this their prayer today.

There is a spirit of offense that is growing more and more prevalent in the world. It causes marriages to end because of "irreconcilable differences," friendships to break down, and relationships to be destroyed. It leads to church splits, petty lawsuits, domestic violence, and even murder.

Recently I was watching the news coverage of a tragic situation that unfolded in my home city of Jacksonville, Florida. Two children got into an argument over who won a basketball game. Instead of just agreeing to disagree and walking away, one child pulled out a gun and shot the other child in the head. How in the world could something like that happen between two kids? The reason we're seeing this more and more is because there is a spirit of offense that has grabbed hold of this world, and it is spreading like wildfire.

As members of the body of Christ, we must guard our

hearts to make sure we don't fall prey to this worldly spirit. We can't allow ourselves to follow the tide of society and become offended at every little thing that does not go our way. Second Corinthians 2:10-11 says, "If you forgive anyone anything, I too forgive that one; and what I have forgiven, if I have forgiven anything, has been for your sakes in the presence [and with the approval] of Christ (the Messiah), to keep Satan from getting the advantage over us; for we are not ignorant of his wiles and intentions" (AMP).

We can't be ignorant of Satan's tactics and fall for his tricks. I believe offense is Satan's number one weapon against Christians. Some people might think fornication is at the top of Satan's list. But if someone commits the sin of fornication and his heart is still open to the Word of God, he can repent and get right with God. When a person gets caught up in offense, however, his heart will often become closed to what the Bible says about forgiveness, and he won't listen to anyone who does not side with him in his hurt.

TWO TYPES OF OFFENSE

Offense is defined as "something that outrages the moral, emotional or physical senses" and "the state of being insulted or morally outraged."[1] Typically, there are two categories of offended people. The first are those who have actually been mistreated.

There are times when things happen to us that are absolutely wrong. For example, when a couple gets married and vows to live together "till death us do part," and for some reason one of them decides to commit adultery or leave, that's just wrong. Now the innocent spouse is left to raise the children, pay the bills, and live alone. Things shouldn't have happened that way. That person has a legitimate reason for feeling hurt.

In the second category are those who *feel* they've been done wrong. These individuals may not have been mistreated at all. In fact, if you brought one hundred reasonable people into a room and gave them the details of the situation, perhaps 90 percent or more would say, "I know you won't like what I'm about to say, but what he did to you really wasn't wrong."

But in these cases it doesn't matter whether the individuals were mistreated or not because their perception becomes their reality. When people feel wronged and don't allow the Holy Spirit to intervene, offense sets in and becomes a deep, dark pit that will prevent them from walking in the miracle-working power of God. Ultimately that is what the enemy intends offense to do—stop the Word of God from working in your life.

Proverbs 18:19 says, "A brother offended is harder to be won over than a strong city, and [their] contentions separate them like the bars of a castle" (AMP). The Bible makes it very clear that when a person gets stuck in offense, it's harder to win him over to a reasonable way of thinking than it is to conquer a fortified city.

During ancient Roman times huge walls surrounded cities. There were soldiers positioned on the wall, always on guard, awaiting an attack. When the children of Israel marched around Jericho for seven days, it was because the walls of the city had to fall down in order for them to take it. Unless God had supernaturally intervened to help them, it would have been nearly impossible for them to invade Jericho and receive their promised land.

Even harder to be won over than a city that has these types of walls and military protection is a brother or sister who has become offended. Proverbs 18:19 goes on to say that their contentions separate them like the bars of a castle. If you think about the bars of a castle or a jail cell, one thing you will note is that they are always parallel. The bars don't bend or give way. They stay the same distance apart, and no matter how much you pull or tug on them, they won't come any closer together.

Just like the bars of that jail cell, the offended person's contentions separate them from the one who offended him. No matter what you say or do, that person won't open his heart enough to come close to reconciling things. That's because a wall is up that says, "I'm offended, I'm mad, and I'm not going to forgive the wrong I feel was done to me! I don't care what you, the minister, or even Jesus Christ has to say! I feel this way, I've got a right to feel this way, and nobody can change that!"

STEALING YOUR FUTURE

We have all been offended and probably know of many others who have been as well. But as a minister of the gospel, I need to warn you that offense is not just some innocent little thing that we can hang on to until we feel like letting go of it. Offense is a serious issue, a weapon designed by the enemy to rob you of God's best and steal the future He has destined for your life.

Offense causes a person to shut down on God's way of handling the problem and urges him to construct walls of safety, which eventually become walls of imprisonment. These walls are built of pride, with a gate that opens only to those who agree with the offended person.

When someone has offended you, do you want to hear what the Bible says about forgiveness? No! Offense's job is to get you to close your ears to God's way of rectifying the situation. Furthermore, you may choose not to interact with the person who offended you and thereby create a pathway of safety to protect yourself from getting hurt again.

But what you meant to be a means of protection will unknowingly become a wall of imprisonment. It will hold you captive and keep you from getting to what God wants you to have.

When you are offended, you view every word people speak through the lens of your hurt, thus cutting off ordinary conversation you should be able to have. The spirit of offense chokes off your ability to give people the benefit of the doubt. It suffocates forgiveness and tolerance. It denies human imperfection. It demands that a simple, loving person be mechanical and precise while trying to express sincerity. It assumes the worst. It ignores obvious intentions and digs around for something ugly and sinister. It allows common, everyday words to be misconstrued.

Offense is quite possibly the most vicious problem in our society today. It nourishes an attitude of dissatisfaction with life, especially among those who choose to carry it around like a badge of honor that reads, "I'm indignant and rightfully so!" Most offended people would rather place the blame on someone else—anyone else—than accept responsibility and acknowledge that it is their choice to be offended.

DON'T SIGN FOR THE PACKAGE

When offense comes on the scene, it's like a UPS or FedEx courier coming to your front door. Just because he shows up, rings your bell, and says he has a package for you doesn't mean you have to sign for it. You can't stop the UPS truck from pulling up in front of your house. You can't keep the FedEx courier from ringing your doorbell. But when you open the door, you can choose whether you'll accept the package.

In the same way we can't stop people from doing and saying things that are hurtful and offensive. But we can choose whether we sign for that offense package and allow it to control our lives or change the course of what God wants us to do.

The thing about giving way to offense is that in doing so, you are giving control of your life over to the person who offended you rather than to God. When you change churches because you were offended, it's not God ordering your steps; it's offense. When you leave your job because you don't like what someone said, you've allowed offense to rob you of a job that has been a blessing to you and your family.

One of the best things you can do when you've been offended is not make any major decisions until you have calmed down and can clearly hear what the Holy Spirit is saying. Some of what people say the Lord told them to do after they were offended wasn't really God speaking; it was offense talking.

Often when they say the Lord told them to do this or that, it's their way of saying, "Shut up! I don't want to hear what you or anybody else has to say about it." They just blanket it with "The Lord told me" because they know most people won't argue with what someone believes God said. But isn't it amazing that the Lord wasn't saying anything about making that decision until *after* they were offended?

When God talks to us, He doesn't use the vehicle of heightened negative emotions. It is nearly impossible to hear what God is really saying when your feelings are hurt. One of the best things *to* do when you've been offended is *to not* do anything differently until you get your emotions under control. Then you can really hear what the Lord is saying to your spirit.

Let me be very clear: I am not trying to convince you that refusing to be offended is an easy task. Satan is very good at his job. He's not going to send someone you barely know to do you wrong. He's going to send those who are closest to you—those you would least expect to hurt you.

Psalm 55:12–14 says, "It is not an enemy who taunts me—I could bear that. It is not my foes who so arrogantly insult me—I could have hidden from them. Instead, it is you—my equal, my companion and close friend. What good fellowship we once enjoyed as we walked together to the house of God" (NLT).

Notice that David said it wasn't some stranger who did him wrong. If it were just somebody out there on the street, he might have been upset for a minute, but eventually he would have forgotten about it. Yet when the person who hurts you is a close friend, it strikes you to the core! David said, "We walked together to the house of God." That means this person went to the same church!

I believe the reason we get so upset by certain things our friends do is because we have a higher expectation of those closest to us. We assume the people at work who don't really know us may do something we don't like, but we don't expect to experience hurt when we come home or go to church. Consequently when people we're in close relationship with do things that don't measure up to our expectations, it tends to cut deeper into our hearts.

This is why you see so many relatives who haven't spoken to one another in years. Offense comes to sever relationships and separate us from the people God has placed in our lives to be a blessing to us—and who we are to bless in return. There is always something that can offend us if we allow it. But when we become mature enough to know that Satan is always going to play the offense card, we can stop his plan to cause us to fail The Offense Test and suffer the consequences.

THE HIGH COST OF OFFENSE

Though Satan will never reveal it to you, there is indeed a price tag for offense. If you go into a clothing store and see a dress or suit that you like, you can't just grab it and walk out. The store has a little camera watching you. There's a guy in a uniform with a whistle, flashlight, and can of mace who will tackle you from behind and detain you until the police come. You can't just walk out without paying what's on the price tag.

Offense also has a price tag associated with it. You can't just partake of offense and think there's no price to pay. The enemy tells you, "Just go ahead and wallow in your offense. Stay right where you are. Put on a good smile and look like nothing is really bothering you." He will never tell you that offense is eating away at the blessing of God. Even if the person really did you wrong, God still does not give you a right to stay angry.

One of the possible costs associated with offense is your

family. Colossians 3:18–21 says, "Wives, be subject to your husbands [subordinate and adapt yourselves to them], as is right and fitting and your proper duty in the Lord. Husbands, love your wives [be affectionate and sympathetic with them] and do not be harsh or bitter or resentful toward them. Children, obey your parents in everything, for this is pleasing to the Lord. Fathers, do not provoke or irritate or fret your children [do not be hard on them or harass them], lest they become discouraged and sullen and morose and feel inferior and frustrated. [Do not break their spirit]" (AMP).

Notice that God has something to say to everybody in the house. He tells the wives to submit to their own husbands. Husbands are to love their wives and not be bitter against them. Children should obey their parents. This information is still important today because many families live in a perpetual state of offense, and it can get so bad that the home looks and feels much like a war zone. Some families attend a good church on a regular basis, lift up their hands and sing songs of praise and worship to God, then go right home and curse out one another. The end result is an entire house full of hostility.

This is not how God wants things to be. The home should be a place of refuge and safety. Prisons are filled with people who come from broken homes and never learned where they could find rest and security. Don't allow the enemy to steal your family by holding on to grudges. Allow God to direct your family life and reap the rewards of obedience.

FORFEITING YOUR MIRACLE

Offense can also cost you your miracle. When Jesus visited His hometown of Nazareth, He couldn't perform any miracles there, and for one reason—offense set in.

> Jesus went away from there and came to His [own] country and hometown [Nazareth], and His disciples followed [with] Him. And on the Sabbath He began to teach in the synagogue; and many who listened to Him were utterly astonished, saying, Where did this Man acquire all this? What is the wisdom [the broad and full intelligence which has been] given to Him? What mighty works and exhibitions of power are wrought by His hands! Is not this the Carpenter, the son of Mary and the brother of James and Joses and Judas and Simon? And are not His sisters here among us? And they took offense at Him and were hurt [that is, they disapproved of Him, and it hindered them from acknowledging His authority] and they were caused to stumble and fall. But Jesus said to them, A prophet is not without honor (deference, reverence) except in his [own] country and among [his] relatives and in his [own] house. And He was not able to do even one work of power there, except that He laid His hands on a few sickly people [and] cured them.
>
> —MARK 6:1–5, AMP

The Bible says these people couldn't receive any miracles because they were offended. Jesus could not overcome the offended hearts of those in His own hometown in order to perform miracles in their lives, and He can't do that for us either.

If we don't want to forfeit the miracle, we have to decide to bypass the offense. A lot of people say, "Oh, if I could just see Jesus! If I could have been there when He walked the streets of Galilee and seen Him raise the dead, I just know I could have believed Him for a miracle."

The truth of the matter is that a lot of Christians today still wouldn't receive a miracle if they saw Jesus face-to-face because they would find Him hard to take. Jesus was a man of business who could sometimes speak in a way that was difficult to hear. One time a Canaanite woman came to Jesus with a serious need.

> And behold, a woman who was a Canaanite from that district came out and, with a [loud, troublesomely urgent] cry, begged, Have mercy on me, O Lord, Son of David! My daughter is miserably and distressingly and cruelly possessed by a demon! But He did not answer her a word. And His disciples came and implored Him, saying, Send her away, for she is crying out after us. He answered, I was sent only to the lost sheep of the house of Israel. But she came and, kneeling, worshiped Him and kept praying, Lord, help me! And He answered, It is not right (proper, becoming, or fair) to take the children's bread and throw it to the little dogs.
> —MATTHEW 15:22–26, AMP

Did Jesus just call this woman a dog? That one statement would have cleared most churches. "Oh, no, He didn't call me a dog! I don't care if that's Jesus or not! Nobody calls *me* a dog!" That's where the offense comes in and steals your miracle.

But this woman passed The Offense Test. Instead of allowing her daughter to continue to be plagued because of her pride, she replied, "Yes, Lord, yet even the little pups (little whelps) eat the crumbs that fall from their [young] masters' table" (Matt. 15:27, AMP). Jesus Himself had to acknowledge her great faith, and He healed her daughter. She received her miracle because she refused to allow offense to take root in her heart.

In the Old Testament we learn about Naaman, who almost failed The Offense Test and lost his healing.

> Now Naaman, captain of the host of the king of Syria, was a great man with his master, and honourable, because by him the LORD had given deliverance unto Syria: he was also a mighty man in valour, but he was a leper.
>
> —2 KINGS 5:1

Naaman had a maid who was from Israel, and she suggested to Naaman's wife that he see the prophet Elisha in order to be healed. Naaman set off for Israel with a letter from the king of Syria, along with silver, gold, and clothes for the king of Israel. When Naaman came to the king of Israel with his letter and presents, the king tore his clothes saying, "Am I God, to kill and to make alive, that this man doth send unto me to recover a man of his leprosy? wherefore consider, I pray you, and see how he seeketh a quarrel against me" (2 Kings 5:7).

When Elisha heard the king had torn his clothes, he told the king not to worry about it. He said, "Let him come now to me, and he shall know there is a prophet in Israel" (v. 8).

> So Naaman came with his horses and with his chariot, and stood at the door of the house of Elisha. And Elisha sent a messenger unto him, saying, Go and wash in Jordan seven times, and thy flesh shall come again to thee, and thou shalt be clean.
>
> —2 KINGS 5:9–10

Naaman was furious! In his anger he spoke two of the most deadly words in the entire Bible: "I thought." Most offense occurs because we "thought" things would be a certain way, but they turned out another way.

> But Naaman was wroth, and went away, and said, Behold, I thought, He will surely come out to me, and stand, and call on the name of the LORD his God, and strike his hand over the place, and recover the leper. Are not Abana and Pharpar, rivers of Damascus, better than all the waters of Israel? may I not wash in them, and be clean? So he turned and went away in a rage.
>
> —2 KINGS 5:11–12

Most offense comes because we have an expectation. When what we expect doesn't pan out, we get offended at the person who didn't do what we wanted him to do: "I thought after going to Bible school I'd be in full-time ministry by now." "After all these years of working at this company, I thought they would have at least interviewed me for that promotion."

Naaman believed his stature and position made him worthy of Elisha's personal attention. He thought Elisha would come out and say, "Oh my goodness, can you believe this? Is that Naaman? I've heard about you, Naaman. Aren't you the one who won that battle over there in Jericho? Oh my goodness!

By the power of the God of Abraham, Isaac, and Jacob, let the leprosy that is upon thee be gone! *Whoosh!*"

Instead Elisha told his servant, "Just go out there. If it's Naaman, I'm expecting him. Tell him to go dip seven times in the Jordan River."

At the beginning of the story we get the impression that all Naaman really wanted was to be healed. But when his healing didn't come the way he anticipated, his real motives were uncovered. Thank God his servants had enough sense to say to him, "Well, Master, if the prophet had told you to go and do something great, wouldn't you have done it so you could be healed?"

If Naaman had not come to his senses, he would have died with leprosy and missed out on precious years with his family. At his funeral people would have been asking, "Why did God let that happen?" They wouldn't have known that God had sent Naaman a way out, and he was too offended to take advantage of it.

But Naaman did listen to his servants. He dipped in the Jordan seven times and came out with brand-new skin! So for Naaman we could say that on the other side of his offense was a miracle—and that is often the case with us. We miss out on all sorts of miracles when we fail The Offense Test.

OFFENDED TO DEATH

The most expensive cost of offense is your life. King Herod had imprisoned John the Baptist because his wife, Herodias, wanted it. John the Baptist had publicly disapproved of Herod's marriage to her since she had been the wife of Herod's brother. Later, during Herod's birthday party, Herodias's daughter performed a dance before the king and his guests that greatly pleased them. So Herod said to the girl:

> Ask of me whatsoever thou wilt, and I will give it thee. And he sware unto her, Whatsoever thou shalt ask of me, I will give it thee, unto the half of my kingdom. And she went forth, and said unto her mother, What shall I ask? And she said, The head of John the Baptist. And she came in straightway with haste unto the king, and asked, saying, I will that thou give me by and by in a charger the head of John the Baptist. And the king was exceeding sorry; yet for his oath's sake, and for their sakes which sat with him, he would not reject her. And immediately the king sent an executioner, and commanded his head to be brought: and he went and beheaded him in the prison, and brought his head in a charger, and gave it to the damsel: and the damsel gave it to her mother.
>
> —Mark 6:22–28

How does someone Jesus described as the greatest man ever born from the womb of a woman end up having his head paraded around on a plate during Herod's drunken party? We know God has the power to rescue people who've been captured. When Daniel was in the lions' den, didn't God demonstrate His power to set him free? When the three Hebrew boys were thrown into a fiery furnace, didn't God demonstrate that He knew how to deliver?

In the New Testament, when the apostles were arrested and thrown in jail, didn't an angel of the Lord come and set them free and tell them, "Go stand right back in the public square and keep on preaching"? When Peter was locked up in jail, didn't an angel of the Lord wake him, break his chains, and send him to the house where the believers were praying the night before the rulers were going to kill him?

So we know God has the ability to set people free who have been captured. Then why did John the Baptist die in such a violent and tragic way? I believe the answer is because he became offended at Jesus.

> John answered them, saying, I baptize with water: but there standeth one among you, whom ye know not; He it is, who coming after me is preferred before me, whose shoe's latchet I am not worthy to unloose. These things were done in Bethabara beyond Jordan, where John was baptizing. The next day John seeth Jesus coming unto him, and saith, Behold the Lamb of God, which taketh away the sin of the world. This is he of whom I said, After me cometh a man which is preferred before me: for he was before me. And I knew him not: but that he should be made manifest to Israel, therefore am I come baptizing with water. And John bare record, saying, I saw the Spirit descending from heaven like a dove, and it abode upon him. And I knew him not: but he that sent me to baptize with water, the same said unto me, Upon whom thou shalt see the Spirit descending, and remaining on him, the same is he which baptizeth with the Holy Ghost. And I saw, and bare record that this is the Son of God.
> —JOHN 1:26–34

John the Baptist had no doubt whatsoever in his mind about who Jesus was. More than once he acknowledged that Jesus was the Lamb of God who came to take away the sin of the world. However, shortly before John was beheaded in prison, he seemed to have some doubts about Jesus.

> And it came to pass, when Jesus had made an end of commanding his twelve disciples, he departed thence to teach and to preach in their cities. Now when John had heard *in the prison* the works of Christ, he sent two of his disciples, and said unto him, Art thou he that should come, or do we look for another?
>
> —MATTHEW 11:1–3, EMPHASIS ADDED

Well, hang on, John! Didn't you say, "Behold! The Lamb of God who takes away the sin of the world"? Didn't you say, "Jesus is the Son of God"? Didn't you acknowledge that He was the Lamb of God? Now, are you sending your disciples to Jesus to ask Him, "Are you the one who is supposed to come, or should we be looking for somebody else?"

The problem is that John has been sitting in prison. And instead of waiting for God's timing for his deliverance, he's sitting in there getting offended because Jesus has not helped him out as he thought He should. Jesus didn't even take time to answer his question.

> Go and shew John again those things which ye do hear and see: The blind receive their sight, and the lame walk, the lepers are cleansed, and the deaf hear, the dead are raised up, and the poor have the gospel preached to them. And blessed is he, whosoever shall not be offended in me.
>
> —MATTHEW 11:4–6

In other words Jesus was telling John, "I'm giving you a chance to recover from this offense." Obviously John didn't heed the warning. You have to know Jesus felt horrible. He must have been wondering, "Why wouldn't this guy listen to Me?"

As a pastor I know that feeling. Why wouldn't this person just listen? Why wouldn't he just open his eyes to see that the offense rooted in his heart is destroying everything God is trying to do in his life? As Jesus did with John, many times I've had to just sit back and watch destruction rain down upon a person's life because he wouldn't open up his heart when God was knocking and asking him to let the offense go.

LOVE NEVER FAILS

Offense is not something you can play around with. It will eat away like a cancer at everything productive in your life unless you release it back to God. When the disciples asked Jesus about His return and the end of the world as we know it, Jesus said that one of the signs of the end times will be widespread offense—"And then shall many be offended, and shall betray one another, and shall hate one another." (See Matthew 24:1–10.)

Offense is a trick of the enemy to trap you. Everywhere you look, somebody is offended or taking out his anger and aggression because he doesn't like something that was done to him. This happens because we live in a time when the spirit of offense won't allow people to put down their guard and let Jesus work it out.

You have to give God room and be willing to say, "You know what? Despite how bad I feel about what happened, I'm willing to let all of this go so the Lord can do what He wants to do in my life." When you call Jesus Lord, it means He has the right to order you to do things you may not want to do.

Sometimes that means having to forgive people and things when your flesh and emotions still want to be riled up. Instead God asks you to choose to be a person who has an attitude and heart like Jesus's. Even when people mistreat you, you love them, forgive them, and let it go for your own benefit.

Agape love, the kind of love God has and that He has placed inside every born-again believer, will not allow you to remain offended. Agape love does not keep score of all of the wrong deeds someone has done.

> Love endures long and is patient and kind; love never is envious nor boils over with jealousy, is not boastful or vainglorious, does not display itself haughtily. It is not conceited (arrogant and inflated with pride); it is not rude (unmannerly) and does not act unbecomingly. Love (God's love in us) does not insist on its own rights or its own way, for it is not self-seeking; it is not touchy or fretful or resentful; it takes no account of the evil done to it [it pays no attention to a suffered wrong]. It does not rejoice at injustice and unrighteousness, but rejoices when right and truth prevail. Love bears up under anything and everything that comes, is ever ready to believe the best of every person, its hopes are fadeless under all circumstances, and it endures everything [without weakening]. Love never fails [never fades out or becomes obsolete or comes to an end].
>
> —1 Corinthians 13:4–8, amp

The only way to get offended and stay offended is if you're keeping track of all the things someone has done to you. The Bible says love is not "touchy or fretful or resentful" (v. 5). The word *touchy* literally means quick to take offense, overly sensitive, requiring special tact or skill in handling, and easily ignited or flammable.

Therefore, if you're a person of love, you can't be easily offended. You can't make people feel like they have to think long and hard about how they're going to talk or act around you to keep from hurting your feelings. You also can't be someone who is easily ignited or flammable; you can't be a stick of dynamite walking around ready to blow up!

THE INFLUENCE OF OUR PERSONALITIES

Knowing your motivational, or spiritual, gifts will help you understand why you think and react to things the way you do. If you don't already know your area of gifting, I recommend you find a good book on motivational gifts and take a spiritual gifts test. This will not only help you discover the area of ministry you are best suited for, but it will also help you see the unique ways offense may try to take root in your life.

Some personality types are more susceptible to offense than others. People with *compassion* and *servant* motivational gifts, for example, tend to be quite sensitive. Because they care so much for people, they can easily get their feelings hurt. They tend to look for little signs of how others feel about them due to their need to be liked or appreciated. If what they believe they see seems less than favorable, they can become upset and think people don't like them or are out to get them. In reality, no one is usually trying to do them any harm at all.

Those with *perceiver* motivational gifts tend to want everything to be just right. They are often *fretful*, which means "irritable," "marked by worry and distress; unable to relax or be still, or moody."[2] Perceivers have a strong urge to have everything fixed. They are not procrastinators; they want things corrected immediately.

The problem with this attitude, of course, is that most things in life don't get fixed right away. You can't put everything in its proper box and make things go exactly the way you want them to all the time. Therefore, perceivers can get offended when circumstances don't fit into their idea of perfection.

Those with *teacher* and *administrator* motivational gifts tend to struggle with feeling resentful when people or things don't make sense to them or are unorganized. *Resent* means "to feel or express annoyance or ill will."[3] To be honest, this is one I have to work on all the time because I have a teacher motivational gift. I'm a law-abiding citizen, except I hate abiding by laws that don't make sense. I do obey those laws, but I can't stand it.

Individuals like me can get annoyed with people simply because they're not doing things that fit our rationale. We get frustrated with people who, in our expert opinion, are not organized. The reason those of us with teacher motivational gifts get irritated is because we think we know everything about everything.

Those who are *exhorters* and *givers*, two other motivational gifts, also can be easily annoyed. When they do things to encourage or bless a person, they need to know they are appreciated. If that appreciation is not present in a big way, they're put off.

All of us have to watch those little areas within our personalities that can make us more prone to offense. Instead of assuming someone has done us wrong, we must remember that the problem may be much closer to home. We may be super-sensitive to particular triggers because of how we're wired.

PASSING THE OFFENSE TEST

As I mentioned before, The Offense Test is the one people fail most often. But the good news is that you *can* pass this test with flying colors if you keep some principles in mind.

1. Admit that you are offended

The first thing you must do to pass The Offense Test is admit it when you are offended. Your feelings are no secret to God. Hebrews 4:12 tells us the Word of God is able to expose, sift, analyze, and judge the very thoughts and purposes of the heart—it exposes us for who we really are.

We can say something didn't bother us, but the Word of God has a way of getting down to the truth of the matter. When God begins to show us where we really are, we then have a choice to get honest with ourselves and allow God's Word to fix us or live in denial. Too many people get offended and refuse to acknowledge it.

This is especially true if they attend a church where they are truly being taught the Word of God. They know they're supposed to walk in love. They know offense is not something they should harbor in their hearts. So they don't want to admit their true state because they know they're violating

God's Word. However, when a person chooses to live in denial, there's nothing anyone can do for him, including Jesus.

How do we determine if we or someone we know is in offense? There are several signs. Offended people tend to have a consistently negative outlook on life. They also tend to be overly critical. They never see the good in anybody. They don't give people the benefit of the doubt. If someone does something that might have been a genuine mistake, they assume the person did it on purpose.

Offended people complain constantly. They may refuse to interact with a particular person. I'm not talking about people who are purposefully trying to get under their skin but those who have asked for forgiveness or who don't realize they did something hurtful. Instead of working out their differences as Matthew 18 teaches, offended people won't have anything to do with the individual they feel wronged them.

Another characteristic of offended people is that they have difficulty getting excited for those they believe wronged them. They have continuous feelings of hurt, anger, or resentment, and will refuse to discuss how to reconcile with the person who upset them.

One of the saddest things about offense is that it negatively affects other relationships that are totally unrelated to the situation that created the offense. That's because offense is like a fungus; it can spread and affect others. The Bible warns us not to allow any root of bitterness to form.

> Strive to live in peace with everybody and pursue that consecration and holiness without which no one will [ever] see the Lord. Exercise foresight and be on the

watch to look [after one another], to see that no one
falls back from and fails to secure God's grace (His
unmerited favor and spiritual blessing), in order that
no root of resentment (rancor, bitterness, or hatred)
shoots forth and causes trouble and bitter torment,
and the many become contaminated and defiled by it.
—HEBREWS 12:14–15, AMP

You probably have seen this in a family in which two siblings are having a dispute. Instead of being mature adults and keeping the dispute quiet, one sibling will talk with family members he's close to, and the other sibling will do the same. Of course each person is going to tell his side of the story, which is skewed by his perspective. When the family members hear the one-sided reports, their hearts will begin to change toward someone who has done nothing to them. Soon there's a feud within the family, and it's all because unresolved conflict between two people contaminated the hearts of others. Now everyone involved is short-circuiting the blessing of the Lord in their lives.

Mothers who have been through terrible divorces can contaminate the hearts of their daughters when they tell them they can't trust any man because all men are dogs. The young lady will grow up without proper respect for her father and men in general. If she doesn't allow God to intervene, she may find herself eventually entering into a marriage that is doomed before it starts because she doesn't know how to respect her husband.

Racism is spread in much the same way. Parents rear their children to believe those of other ethnic groups are not to be trusted and should not be viewed as their equals. Typically this is all because of one bad experience the parents—or the parents' parents—had with someone of another ethnic group. For that reason the children grow up without experiencing the beauty of interacting with and learning about people from other cultures.

God created all of us to be instruments of His love. Offense and God's love cannot coexist. That is why offense has to be acknowledged and uprooted—so it does not spread to others.

2. Resist pride

The second thing you must do to pass The Offense Test is refuse to let pride dictate how you will react. "By pride comes nothing but strife" (Prov. 13:10, NKJV). If strife comes as a result of pride, we must conclude that when a person refuses to let go of offense, pride has grabbed hold of him.

Have you ever heard a person say things such as, "I have more experience. How did he get the job?" Or, "I'm older than he is, and I know more than he does. Who is he to correct me?" This is pride. We give offense an open door when we start to believe we are due certain benefits simply because we've had certain experiences, earned a college degree, or have a title in front of our names.

If anyone deserved to react to not being treated the way He deserved, it would have been Jesus. Jesus was spat upon, spoken evil of, and beaten, though He was the Son of God. Yet the Bible says Jesus made Himself of no reputation. He had all the status any person could ever dream of, but He never felt it was above Him to wash His disciples' feet. When you come with the mind-set of a servant, it's hard to get offended.

3. Decide to forgive

The third thing you need to do to pass The Offense Test is make a quality decision to forgive the person or people who offended you. The Bible says, "For if you forgive people their trespasses [their reckless and willful sins, leaving them, letting them go, and giving up resentment], your heavenly Father will also forgive you. But if you do not forgive others their trespasses [their reckless and willful sins, leaving them, letting them go, and giving up resentment], neither will your Father forgive you your trespasses" (Matt. 6:14–15, AMP).

All of us need forgiveness, even after we have given our lives to Christ. In this passage in Matthew 6 Jesus is letting us know that if we are to be partakers of God's forgiveness, we also must be dispensers of it. That means we have to let go of the resentment, bitterness, and hurt—even if we were purposely wronged. No matter what the intentions of the person who hurt us, we must forgive and commend him to God. We don't do this by expecting God to heap punishment upon the person, but by having the same heart of love Jesus had on the cross when He asked God to forgive His offenders.

God is so long-suffering that even when somebody is absolutely wrong, He often will give him time to turn around and make things right. We needed the grace of God to abound toward us when we were blatantly wrong, and we need to extend that same grace to others as proponents of God's love. In doing this, we will not only bless the person we forgive, but we also will be blessed.

Life is terrible, lonely, and cold when you're bitter. But there is beauty in forgiveness. Forgiveness is not an emotion. You don't have to feel like forgiving someone. Forgiveness is a decision. It is an act of your will.

When you forgive someone, you are choosing not to expect anything from the person as restitution for what he did wrong. You are deciding to restore him to a place in your heart where you can love and pray for him just as you would anybody else.

That does not mean you become best friends with the person, but it means you're not going to harbor bitterness and ill will in your heart toward him. And if there is ever an opportunity for you to be a blessing to that person, you should take advantage of it, as you would choose to bless anyone else who came your way. There is a freedom that comes from living without unforgiveness in your heart and knowing you've done what Jesus Himself would do.

4. Pray

Jesus said, "But I say unto you which hear, Love your enemies, do good to them which hate you, bless them that curse you, and pray for them which despitefully use you" (Luke 6:27–28). If you want to pass The Offense Test, you must pray for the person who offended you.

When people tell you someone is saying negative things about you, it is natural to become upset. But when someone is saying all kinds of evil things about you, Jesus says you should bless him, say good things about him, and pray for him. It's hard to stay offended with somebody when you are praying for him.

Jesus goes on to tell us that if we love or do nice things only for those who love and do nice things for us, we're no better than those who don't know Jesus. Instead we should love and be good to our enemies without expecting anything in return. If we do this, our reward will be great, and everyone will be able to see that we are children of God because we have shown His character through our conduct. (See Luke 6:30–36.)

I'd say that 99 percent of the time, when a person stays offended with someone, it is because he has not been praying for that person. You cannot consistently pray sincerely for someone and stay offended at the same time. It's not possible. There's something about genuinely asking God to pour His blessings into a person's life that softens our hearts.

5. Remember your miracle

The fifth thing you need to do to pass The Offense Test is to remind yourself of the miracle that awaits you beyond the offense. That's how the Canaanite woman received the healing she needed for her daughter. Jesus told her He shouldn't take the anointing intended to bless the children of Israel and give it to those who were not God's chosen people. But this woman kept her focus on the fact that Jesus was the answer to her daughter's problem.

If she could only get Jesus to agree to make her daughter well, everything would be all right. So that became her anchor. It kept her from becoming offended at Jesus's statement and gave her the strength to ask for just a morsel of His power to make her daughter well.

That's true for you as well. A miracle is waiting for you on the other side of your offense. Maybe it's a miracle of healing. Maybe it's peace in your mind. Maybe it's that child coming back home. Whatever the miracle may be, you have a choice to make. You can remain offended, or you choose to release the offense and claim what's yours!

6. Identify the lessons you need to learn

The final thing you need to do to pass The Offense Test is to identify the character lessons you need to learn. The Bible says, "Therefore I always exercise and discipline myself [mortifying my body, deadening my carnal affections, bodily appetites, and worldly desires, endeavoring in all respects] to have a clear (unshaken, blameless) conscience, void of offense toward God and toward men" (Acts 24:16, AMP).

After you've owned up to the fact that you're offended and refused to let pride tell you how you should react, after you've made a quality decision to forgive and committed to pray for the person who offended you, once you've reminded yourself of the miracle that's awaiting you on the other side of that offense, your next step is to identify the character lessons you need to learn about yourself.

Even if you were truly wronged, the Lord will still use the situation to teach you some lessons if you are open to it. Perhaps He'll tell you, "Yes, that person did you wrong, but you could have responded differently." If we learn the lesson this time, then the next time The Offense Test comes—and you can be sure it will come again—you will be prepared to respond in a way that honors the Lord. You'll pass the test without much effort, and you'll be so proud of yourself!

Why don't you just take a moment right now to humble yourself and ask the Lord to show you if someone or something has offended you. Maybe it's an organization or your job. Maybe it's your spouse, your parents, or your pastor. Has someone come to mind, someone you took offense with or who tempted you to take offense?

If the Lord is speaking to you about someone, I urge you to not let another day go by with offense brewing in your heart. If left unchecked, it will turn into bitterness. Ask God to stir your heart with compassion and genuine love, so you can see the good in the person, just as He does. Ask Him to give you the strength to pass The Offense Test by walking in total forgiveness toward everyone who has sinned against you.

DISCUSSION STARTERS

1. Has The Offense Test been difficult for you in the past? How so?

2. Is there a particular area that tends to leave you easily offended? If so, what do you think this means?

3. Which of the six steps will help you in passing The Offense Test the next time you have to take it?

4. Can you think of a time when you failed The Offense Test? What did you learn about yourself from that failure?

Chapter Eleven

The GRATITUDE TEST

*The Gratitude Test shows whether you will give God thanks
for what He's done with the same passion you had when
you were asking for His help. Passing this test touches the
heart of your Father, leaving Him ready to do more in
your life. And saying thanks reminds you of just how good
God has been to you despite the challenges you faced.*

I SAW A PROGRAM on the Discovery Channel recently that showed modern examples of people who are living with leprosy. If you know anything about leprosy, you know it's an absolutely hideous disease. It was destroying the bodies of the men on this program—so much so that many of them had to have their toes amputated. When I saw how terribly people suffer with this disease and the pain leprosy causes, it really drove home a story in the Bible about Jesus's encounter with ten men who were lepers.

> And it came to pass, as he went to Jerusalem, that he passed through the midst of Samaria and Galilee. And as he entered into a certain village, there met him ten men that were lepers, which stood afar off: and they lifted up their voices, and said, Jesus, Master, have mercy on us. And when he saw them, he said unto them, Go shew yourselves unto the priests. And it came to pass, that, as they went, they were cleansed. And one of them, when he saw that he was healed, turned back, and with a loud voice glorified God, and fell down on his face at his feet, giving him thanks: and he was a Samaritan. And Jesus answering said, Were there not ten cleansed? but where are the nine? There are not found that returned to give glory to God, save this stranger.
>
> —LUKE 17:11–18

These ten men are standing there, screaming out to Jesus, "Son of David, have mercy on us! Please do something to help us!" Jesus tells them, "Go show yourself to the priests." They gather up enough faith to head in the direction of the house of the priests, and as they are going toward the priests' house, the Bible says they are "cleansed." Their leprosy disappears. Their skin returns to normal, and their bodies look and feel as good as new.

Then one of the men turns around and goes back, and with a loud voice he begins to thank Jesus over and over and over. The Amplified Bible says it this way:

> Then one of them, upon seeing that he was cured, turned back, recognizing and thanking and praising

God with a loud voice; and he fell prostrate at Jesus' feet, thanking him [over and over]. And he was a Samaritan. Then Jesus asked, Were not [all] ten cleansed? Where are the nine? Was there no one found to return and to recognize and give thanks and praise to God except for this alien?

—LUKE 17:15–18

This guy was so grateful that he wouldn't have to live the rest of his life with leprosy he couldn't go straight to the priest to get it confirmed. He couldn't rush to tell his wife about it. He couldn't go and show off to his family and friends. He couldn't start doing all the things he wasn't able to do before.

He couldn't do any of those things until he first went back to Jesus to express his gratitude. He was just too thankful to do anything else before he fell down at Jesus's feet and said, "Thank You, Jesus." He said it over and over and over. This one man—an alien, a foreigner—was the only one of the ten who passed what I call *The Gratitude Test*.

The Gratitude Test shows whether you will give God thanks for what He's done with the same passion you had when you were asking for His help. Passing this test touches the heart of your Father, leaving Him ready to do more in your life. And saying thanks reminds you of just how good God has been to you despite the challenges you faced.

You know how passionate you get when you're asking God to do something. "Come on, Lord!" you say. "Send Your power, Lord! Do this thing!"

That's how these men were too. They were crying out so loudly they stopped Jesus's caravan, and He came over to help.

But when they received what they wanted from Jesus, they went on their way. I'm not saying they weren't grateful. I'm not saying they didn't have thanks in their hearts. But they didn't let Jesus know how grateful they were; they kept going.

Nine of these ten men failed The Gratitude Test—that's 90 percent! I believe this story is in the Bible for a reason. I believe God is showing us that this is true for 90 percent of Christians these days too.

I submit to you that 90 percent of the time we fail The Gratitude Test. We receive something from God, but 90 percent of the time we don't come back and thank Him with the same passion we had when we were asking Him to answer our prayer.

I'm not saying we don't thank God at all. I'm not saying we don't have gratitude in our hearts. But our level of thankfulness usually doesn't come close to how passionate we are when we're crying out to God, when we're asking Him to move this mountain or turn this situation around.

We need to be just as fervent in expressing our gratitude to Him. The Gratitude Test says if we spent ten days fasting and praying and believing God for something, we need to set aside at least one day to do nothing but thank God for answering our prayer.

AN ATTITUDE OF GRATITUDE

If we were to sit down and look at where our lives are today compared to where we might have been if the Lord hadn't been so good, we could spend the rest of the year—twenty-four hours a day, every single second of the day—giving thanks and praise to God.

176

Whether you realize it or not, God has been good to you. You might not have everything you want. You might not have everything you need. There may be a long laundry list of things you're still believing God for, but God has been good to you. He has been right there, walking with you every step of the way. And now it's time to turn around and tell Him, "I remember how good You've been! I remember what things were like before You showed up! I have come back just to say, Thank You, Lord! Hallelujah!"

It's time to start passing this Gratitude Test. Passing this test is the key to getting over—and staying over—depression. Too many Christians go through bouts of depression. Even as a pastor I have had to deal with this from time to time. For me part of the problem is that I set such high expectations for myself. Part of it is that I carry the responsibility of so many people.

I have to constantly make sure I stay focused on what the Lord is saying and not let myself get dragged into feeling discouraged about things. When I look around at my life, even when everything might not be exactly the way I like it, I know I have a good life. God has been good to me!

God has been good to you too. One of the best ways to keep from becoming depressed is to remind yourself of God's faithfulness. When you look around and start counting the blessings that are already evident in your life, you'll realize that though some things may not be quite the way you want them to be, God has still been so good to you.

Second Timothy 3:1 says in the last days "perilous times shall come." And one of the things that will happen at that time is that men will become "unthankful" (v. 2). People won't be grateful to God, and they won't be thankful for things other human beings have done for them. They'll have an "entitlement mentality," where they feel others are supposed to do things for them.

We see a lot of that going on today, don't we? We see that especially with many of our young people. A lot of them seem to think they are owed something. Some of that attitude is a result of mistakes made in the way they've been reared, but much of it is a demonic spirit that is becoming prevalent in these last days.

What I'm referring to is a spirit of unthankfulness that is hovering over the world. It even tries to hover over the body of Christ. If we don't watch out, Christians too will slip into this mind-set of forgetting to thank God for how good He has been.

Every year at Thanksgiving we slow down to remind ourselves of what God has done, but every day ought to be Thanksgiving for Christians! When the world celebrates Thanksgiving, we should be celebrating with them as the culmination of all the thanks we've been giving God the whole year.

When you start living your life on purpose by constantly giving thanks to God, then you won't have as much time to fret about the things that aren't going quite the way you want them to.

THANKING GOD IN EVERY SITUATION

First Thessalonians 5:16–18 says, "Rejoice evermore. Pray without ceasing. In every thing give thanks: for this is the will of God in Christ Jesus concerning you." What does it say is the will of God for us? That we thank God in everything. No matter what our circumstances may be, we should be appreciative and give God thanks.

Notice that the Word says "*in* everything give thanks." There's a big difference between *in* everything give thanks and *for* everything give thanks. I heard a TV preacher talk about this verse not long ago. He said, "If cancer has hit your body, you ought to thank God for that cancer."

"Preacher," I said to the TV, "you are out of your mind!" You don't thank God for cancer. That would be like you thanking me for a bag of rotten eggs someone gave you in the church parking lot. I'd turn around and say, "Don't thank me for that. I didn't give that to you."

If you were to thank God for cancer, you'd be saying He was the one who gave it to you, or that He somehow orchestrated your developing cancer, or that He opened the door and gave the devil permission to give you that cancer. God loves you too much to give you something as evil as cancer. I love my children, and no matter how disobedient they could ever be, even if they had broken everything in the house, I would never put cancer on them to teach them a lesson.

At my previous church in Detroit I was the visitation minister, and I loved that position. Many times I'd go to the hospital and visit people who had been in a car accident. They'd say things like, "I thank God for allowing me to have this car accident, because He wanted to get my attention and slow me down. Since I've been in this hospital bed, oh, I've been worshiping God."

Most times I'd give them enough time to get out and get home before I would gently correct them. "Well, thank God

He protected you in that car accident," I'd say. "But God did not initiate that car accident to put you in the hospital so He could talk with you. Honestly, He's been trying to talk with you all along, and if you had just slowed down long enough to listen, you might even have heard Him say, 'Turn left at that light,' and you may have avoided that car accident completely."

So many times we have these religious ways of thinking that have come from things we heard somebody say at some point in our lives. If we don't watch it, we can start forming our beliefs through that filter—and end up thanking God for something He had nothing to do with.

God is not going to take your child or your spouse away from you. Even if your spouse is a disobedient unbeliever who doesn't want anything to do with Christianity, God loves your spouse too much to just write him or her off. He sent Jesus Christ to shed His blood so your spouse would turn around. Now, your spouse may have been living in disobedience, which left a door wide open that the enemy could use to take his or her life. But God always errs on the side of love—He'll never be the one who takes your spouse away.

Yet the Word does say, "In every thing give thanks" (1 Thess. 5:18). In every situation we find ourselves in, we must give thanks to God. I'm not thanking Him for this sickness, but I'm thanking Him that in the midst of this sickness He's still with me. I'm not thanking Him for this divorce, but I'm thanking Him that in the midst of this divorce, when others would have lost their minds and been unable to handle the situation, I know I'm still going to be all right.

I'm not thanking God for the problems in my family, but I'm thanking Him that in the midst of it all, this is not the end for me. I'm thanking Him that as long as I still have breath in my body this thing is not over yet. I'm thanking Him in the middle of it all. I'm thanking Him while bills are stacked up on the table and my mind is telling me there's no way I'll ever get them paid. I'm thanking Him right there in the middle of the situation instead of crying and giving up.

Instead of saying God doesn't love me or that everything always goes wrong for me, I'm going to use that time and energy to thank God. "I thank You, Lord. You are still my Jehovah Jireh. I thank You, Lord. You are still El Shaddai. You are still the One who supplies my every need. You are still the One who has a sudden good break with my name on it, and it just might be today when this thing gets turned around!"

FIGHTING THE GOOD FIGHT OF FAITH

Having an attitude of gratitude causes you to look at your problems and realize they might be problems today, but they'll soon be praise reports. Every praise report you've ever heard began as a problem. It can't become a praise report until it has been a problem first, and you've got to learn how to give thanks to God despite what the situation looks like.

"I have been young, and now am old," David said, "yet have I not seen the righteous forsaken, nor his seed begging bread" (Ps. 37:25). David was saying, "I've always seen God come through for the righteous person." God may not come through right when you wanted Him to, but He's always on time. He'll always make sure that at the right time, in the right moment, and in just the right season, what you need will be right where you need it to be.

So you must know how to praise your way through the

situation, to dance when you don't feel like dancing and to rejoice when you don't want to rejoice. This is what it means to fight the good fight of faith. You don't feel like doing it, yet you do it anyway. And you keep doing it until you see the breakthrough God has promised.

You'll find there's something about witnessing a breakthrough. All it takes is seeing God demonstrate His faithfulness one time. It changes you. You gain a new confidence. You develop an attitude that is convinced God is going to come through, and no one can tell you otherwise.

SLOPPILY PROSPEROUS

After Moses led the children of Israel out of Egypt, he gathered all the people together and warned them in Deuteronomy 8 to be careful not to flunk The Gratitude Test. He began by saying, "For the LORD thy God..." (v. 7). Sometimes you have to remind yourself that He's your God. You have to tell yourself, "I know He's God to the whole world, but He's also *my* God—He's my Father God."

Moses told the people, "For the LORD thy God bringeth thee into a good land..." God is trying to bring you to a good land too. If you look around right now and your life doesn't look like a good land, don't stop walking, because you're not there yet. Don't stop, because God says He's bringing you into a good land. And when you arrive in that place, there will be no denying it. You'll look around and declare, "I am living in a good land!"

Moses said the good land was "a land of brooks of water, of fountains and depths that spring out of valleys and hills; a land of wheat, and barley, and vines, and fig trees, and pomegranates; a land of oil olive, and honey; a land wherein thou shalt eat bread without scarceness, thou shalt not lack any thing in it; a land whose stones are iron, and out of whose hills thou mayest dig brass. When thou hast eaten and art full, then thou shalt bless the LORD thy God for the good land which he hath given thee. Beware that thou forget not the LORD thy God" (vv. 8–11).

"Beware," Moses said. This is The Gratitude Test. *"Beware that thou forget not the LORD thy God..."* What we have to watch for is that when God brings us closer to that land—when He starts filling us up, when He starts turning our sorrow into joy, our mourning into dancing—we don't forget to thank Him the way we did when we didn't have anything.

There's a real temptation to become what I call "sloppily prosperous." This is when God has blessed you to a point where you don't have to believe God every month for the rent or mortgage to get paid, and you start to get careless about thanking Him. The Lord dealt with me about this a few years ago. He told me I had become sloppy, that I wasn't coming back to Him and giving Him the same level of thanks and praise for the "little things" as I used to back in the day. He reminded me that I have to slow down and remember to thank Him for every blessing, large and small.

Moses ended his warning by saying:

> Beware that thou forget not the LORD thy God, in not keeping his commandments, and his judgments, and his statutes, which I command thee this day: Lest when thou hast eaten and art full, and hast built goodly houses, and dwelt therein; and when thy herds and thy

flocks multiply, and thy silver and gold is multiplied, and all that thou hast is multiplied; then thine heart be lifted up, and thou forget the LORD thy God, which brought thee forth out of the land of Egypt, from the house of bondage; who led thee through that great and terrible wilderness, wherein were fiery serpents, and scorpions, and drought, where there was no water; who brought thee forth water out of the rock of flint; who fed thee in the wilderness with manna, which thy fathers knew not, that he might humble thee, and that he might prove thee, to do thee good at thy latter end; and thou say in thine heart, My power and the might of mine hand hath gotten me this wealth. But thou shalt remember the LORD thy God: for it is he that giveth thee power to get wealth, that he may establish his covenant which he sware unto thy fathers, as it is this day.

—DEUTERONOMY 8:11–18

Notice that God was saying to the people: "As I start blessing and prospering you, make sure you don't get it twisted and start thinking your education got this done for you. Make sure you don't get it upside down and think your talent is the reason you're succeeding." He says, "Remember that I am the One who has given you power to get wealth."

This goes beyond just financial wealth. God is the one who gives us the power to succeed. He says we must be sure to turn around and give proper thanks to the One who deserves the respect and the praise for every good thing that happens in our lives.

BUILD A MEMORIAL

One of the things you'll notice about the children of Israel is that they were constantly forgetting what God had already done for them. Every time some new problem came up in their lives—they were trapped at the Red Sea, they didn't have enough food, they didn't have enough water—they'd start to panic, turn on God, and turn on Moses. And the reason they were turning on God and turning on Moses is because they failed to remember what God had done for them.

Therefore God constantly told them to build memorials. Every time He delivered them by doing something mighty and tremendous in their lives, He would tell them, "Stop and make a memorial in this place. Designate this spot in your lives so that when you pass by again, there will be something here to jar your memory and remind you of the great things I've done. And not only will this memorial remind you of what I've done, but after you're dead and gone, it will remind your children and your grandchildren that I have been good to this family for a long time."

In Exodus 3, when God first spoke to Moses in the burning bush about going into Egypt to rescue His people, Moses said, "Who am I that I should go unto Pharaoh, and that I should bring forth the children of Israel out of Egypt?"

God replied by saying, "Certainly I will be with thee; and this shall be a token unto you that I have sent thee, that I have sent thee: When thou hast brought forth the people out of Egypt, ye shall serve God upon this mountain."

Then Moses asked, "Behold, when I come unto the children of Israel, and shall say unto them, The God of your fathers hath sent me unto you; and they shall say to me, What is his name? what shall I say unto them?"

"I AM THAT I AM," God said. "Thus shalt thou say unto the children of Israel, I AM hath sent me unto you."

God went on to say, "Thus shalt thou say unto the children of Israel, the LORD God of your fathers, the God of Abraham, the God of Isaac, and the God of Jacob, hath sent me unto you: this is my name for ever and this is my memorial unto all generations" (Exod. 3:11–15).

God was telling Moses, "I want you to mark the spot where you're standing right now because this is going to be a sign to you that I have done exactly what I told you I would do. Once I've sent you into Egypt with my name to deliver the children of Israel, you're going to come back past this spot. And when you see this spot that you've marked, it's going to remind you of My words, and you're going to say, "Oh yeah, He did exactly what He told me He was going to do!"

This is one of the things you have to learn how to do in your life. You must mark the spot where God delivered you. You must mark the spot where that child got saved or that spouse turned to the Lord.

I've told the story many times about how God transformed my life when I was a seventeen-year-old kid at Cass Tech High School in Detroit. I had been going to church my whole life, but I wasn't saved. I was the director of the Cass Tech Gospel Choir and wasn't saved. But then one Monday morning, a guy in the choir came into the auditorium where we used to rehearse before school, and he began talking about how we need to live right before God. He said if we were going to be up there singing for God, we couldn't be living any kind of way.

I had heard that many times before, but for some reason on that day it registered in my heart in a way it hadn't before. It affected me so deeply I didn't even go to class that day. One of my good friends and I left the school and went to my house. And as the two of us sat there at my kitchen table, I gave my heart to the Lord. That moment is just as clear to me today as it was when it happened. Why is that? Because I marked that spot. That's a memorial in my life.

A couple of months later the Cass Tech Gospel Choir hosted a big concert series at the end of the year, and we went to different churches across the city to sing. I remember during one of our performances I was standing there praising God with my hands up in the air. I was a young Baptist boy who had grown up in the Baptist church his whole life, but as I was worshiping God that day, out of my mouth came these words that I had never spoken before, and I began speaking in other tongues.

I wasn't expecting it, and as far as I knew I had never in my life heard anybody speak in tongues. To this day I remember that moment like it happened yesterday. Why? Because I have marked that spot in my life as a memorial.

In the personal planner I carry around with me, I have marked the anniversary of the day I was born again and the anniversary of the day I was filled with the Holy Ghost. Every year when those dates roll around, I look down at my calendar and am reminded that God has been good to me for a long time.

This is what God was saying to Moses: "Mark this spot right

here because when you come back by, it will remind you that I have done exactly what I told you I was going to do."

So I want to encourage you to start marking some spots in your life. Build yourself some memorials. Sometimes the reason it looks like this new giant you're facing today is so big is because you have forgotten how many giants God has already slain in your life. But when you've marked the spot and you can go back to remind yourself of what God has done for you already, you won't be intimidated by some new giant. You'll realize that it's just a new giant with a new name and that you still serve the same God.

WRITE A BOOK ABOUT IT

In Exodus 17 the children of Israel had just come out of Egypt and were still wandering in the wilderness when the Amalekites decided to come up and attack them.

> Then came Amalek, and fought with Israel in Rephidim. And Moses said unto Joshua, Choose us out men, and go out, fight with Amalek: to morrow I will stand on the top of the hill with the rod of God in mine hand. So Joshua did as Moses had said to him and fought with Amalek: and Moses, Aaron and Hur went up to the top of the hill. And it came to pass, when Moses held up his hand, that Israel prevailed: and when he let down his hand, Amalek prevailed. But Moses' hands were heavy; and they took a stone, and put it under him, and he sat thereon; and Aaron and Hur stayed up his hands, the one on the one side, the other on the other side; and his hands were steady until the going down of the sun. And Joshua discomfited Amalek and

his people with the edge of the sword. And the LORD
said unto Moses, Write this for a memorial in a book.

—EXODUS 17:8–14

Notice that God is telling Moses again, "Don't forget what
just happened." Then He said, "Write this for a memorial in
a book, and rehearse it in the ears of Joshua: for I will utterly
put out the remembrance of Amalek from under heaven. And
Moses built an altar, and called the name of it Jehovah-nissi
[which means "the Lord is my banner"]" (Exod. 17:14–15).

When the Amalekites attacked them, the Israelites weren't
an army. They had just come out of Egypt, where they had
been slaves for four hundred years. They weren't accustomed to fighting. They were accustomed to serving. So the
Amalekites tried to take advantage of the Israelites while they
were in a vulnerable place, but God stepped in to do the seem-
ingly impossible on behalf of His people.

Moses recognized that they didn't win this battle because
they were skilled at fighting. They didn't get to where they
were because of their intellect or their might. They got there
for one reason—the Lord was on their side.

In times of war the flag or the banner is raised as the ral-
lying point for the troops. When everyone in the company
sees that flag or banner, they know the direction the company is going in, and they are encouraged by the symbol of
what they're fighting for. Moses recognized that the Israelites
were not winning the battle because of their own strength or
strategy. He acknowledged that they were prevailing because
Jehovah was their banner, so he built an altar. He marked the
spot and called that place *Jehovah-nissi.*

We need to go back and start identifying the spots where the Lord delivered us—"I wouldn't have gotten through that terrible mess if the Lord hadn't been my banner." "I wouldn't be on this job if the Lord hadn't been my banner." "I wouldn't have had another opportunity if the Lord had not been my banner." We have to go back and mark those places in our lives.

If you're going to pass The Gratitude Test, you must do this. You have to go back and mark that spot where the enemy could have taken you out, but the Lord became your shield and your buckler. Go back and mark the spot where you could have thrown in the towel if the Lord hadn't given you the strength to keep on going. Go back and mark that spot in your life. And when you do, it will always be there to remind you that if He did it before, He will do it again.

After Moses died, Joshua began to lead the people of Israel. God was preparing them to finally enter the Promised Land, but they faced a pretty significant obstacle: the Jordan River. God reminded them of how He had parted the Red Sea when He delivered them out of Egypt, and He promised to deliver them again. God kept His word and parted the Jordan so the children of Israel could pass over on dry ground. After He brought them through, God gave the people specific instructions.

> It came to pass, when all the people were clean passed over Jordan, that the LORD spake unto Joshua saying, Take you twelve men out of the people, out of every tribe a man, and command ye them, saying, Take you hence out of the midst of Jordan, out of the place where the

priests' feet stood firm, twelve stones, and ye shall carry them over with you, and leave them in the lodging place, where you shall lodge this night. Then Joshua called the twelve men, whom he had prepared of the children of Israel, out of every tribe a man: And Joshua said unto them, Pass over before the ark of the LORD your God into the midst of Jordan, and take you up every man of you a stone upon his shoulder, according to the number of the tribes of the children of Israel: That this may be a sign among you, that when your children ask their fathers in time to come, saying, What mean ye by these stones? Then ye shall answer them, That the waters of Jordan were cut off before the ark of the covenant of the LORD; when it passed over Jordan, the waters of Jordan were cut off: and these stones shall be for a memorial unto the children of Israel for ever.

—JOSHUA 4:1–7

Notice God is telling them again, "I want you to leave something right here that is going to remind you of what I've done for you."

MAKING GOD BIG

These were just three times when God asked His people to build memorials. You can go through the Bible and easily find ten or fifteen more instances where God told His people to build a memorial here or an altar there. There are also times when Moses—or Abraham or Isaac or Jacob—took it upon himself to build an altar as a place of remembrance.

Apparently God's people have short memories because He kept telling them to build something so they don't forget what

He has done. If their memories weren't so bad, He may have just told them to make sure they remembered what He'd done for them. Instead He tells them, "Leave something right here as physical evidence, so that when you pass by this way again, everybody will stop and ask themselves, 'Why is this big heap of stones right here?'"

Then later when they passed the place, someone would turn around and say, "That's the spot where God told the priests, 'As soon as your feet step into the waters, I'm going to open up these waters for you.'" And then they would all be reminded to praise God for the great things He has done.

God wants us to be able to recount what He's done for us. And when we start recounting what He's done, we won't be able to help but express our gratitude to Him. Psalm 69:30–31 says, "I will praise the name of God with a song, and will magnify him with thanksgiving. This also shall please the LORD better than an ox or bullock that hath horns and hoofs."

The writer says, "I will magnify Him with thanksgiving." In other words, "I will make God big with my thanksgiving. I'll talk about how good He has been to me by thanking Him for what He's done." The psalmist then says, "This is going to please God better than—not just as much as, but *better than*—the sacrifice of an ox or a bull."

Back during Old Testament days God's people ordinarily would bring an ox or a bullock to sacrifice to the Lord. But the psalmist is saying his thanksgiving is more pleasing to God than an animal sacrifice. Why? Because someone could bring an ox or a bullock from the field, but that doesn't mean his heart is in it. Someone could bring his tithe and offering, but that doesn't mean his heart is in it.

There are some people who bring their tithe and offering superstitiously, not to honor God but because they don't want a curse to come upon them. They tithe or give an offering to make sure things go well for them. That is not what pleases the Lord.

Psalm 69:30 says, "I will praise the name of God with a song, and will magnify him with thanksgiving." When we open up our mouths and begin singing a song unto God and offering Him thanksgiving, it pleases Him even more than our gifts. Why? Because we can't thank God without reaching down into our hearts.

In order to thank God, we have to remember. So we must stop and reflect. We could write out a check without even thinking about it. We could reach into our wallets or purses and put something into the offering bucket without ever considering how good God has been. But in order to really give thanks, we have to stop and think, "What am I thanking Him for?" And when we do this, it reminds us that God has been good to us for a long time.

THE SACRIFICE OF GRATITUDE

Thanksgiving is better than a sacrifice, and sometimes thanksgiving is a sacrifice. Psalm 107:21–22 says, "Oh that men would praise the LORD for his goodness, and for his wonderful works to the children of men! And let them sacrifice the sacrifices of thanksgiving, and declare his works with rejoicing."

Sometimes, when things aren't going quite the way we want, it's a sacrifice to thank God. Our minds tend to get stuck on whatever is not working out right. Have you ever noticed in yourself a tendency to drift toward the negative instead of the positive? You can have fifty things going right and one thing going wrong, and your mind will keep going back to that one bad thing instead of the fifty good things. That's when thanksgiving feels like a sacrifice.

But you'll always pass The Gratitude Test when you thank God with the same passion you had when you were asking Him to meet your need. Sometimes that means you have to make yourself express gratitude to God. You may not feel well right now. You may not feel like singing right now. You may not feel like getting on your knees right now. But you have to do it anyway. You have to tell your body to just do it.

God has been too good for you to sit there and give thanks to God with a little quiet voice. You don't pass The Gratitude Test with a whisper—you pass it with rejoicing and a shout!

DISCUSSION STARTERS

1. What are some of the benefits of passing The Gratitude Test?

2. What are some of the times in your life when God has come through for you? Did you build a memorial? If not, how can you do so today?

3. Can you think of a time in your life when it felt like a sacrifice to thank God? Did you thank and praise Him as you should have?

4. What do you believe would be a sign that you're passing The Gratitude Test?

Chapter Twelve

The PERFECT STORM

The Perfect Storm will test the authenticity of your relationship with Christ. And it will reveal what you will do when the winds of controversy, disappointment, confrontation, misunderstanding, delay, distraction, and pressure all seem to collide on your life at the same time.

This test is the grandfather of all tests, and it is Satan's last-ditch effort to keep you from obtaining the blessing that is about to hit your life with a vengeance, if you can only muster up the strength to stay the course and remain faithful to Word of God.

YOU MAY HAVE seen a movie called *The Perfect Storm*. Based on true events, the film involves, as you might guess, a big storm. In late October 1991, a nor'easter with hurricane-force winds formed off the coast of Massachusetts and merged with cold air flowing down from the Arctic and warm air and moisture flowing up from the Gulf Stream. The rare collision of these three weather systems created what meteorologists call a "perfect" storm, and it brought disastrous consequences for commercial fisherman Billy Tyne and his five-man crew on the *Andrea Gail*.

A "perfect" storm results in nature when a series of powerful meteorological events occur simultaneously to create an exceptionally strong storm. Although each weather system is significant on its own, it is the combination of these events that produces devastating hurricane-like conditions.

A "perfect storm" can hit the lives of believers too. This happens when a series of tests occur simultaneously to create an exceptionally powerful test. For example, one day something bad may happen, and all of a sudden we have to deal with The Disappointment Test. We've been disappointed before and figure we can handle that one. But then somebody comes along and says something derogatory, and now we're also facing The Confrontation Test. And if their comments are particularly hurtful, add The Offense Test.

It's one thing to be under pressure at home or work. It's another thing to be under pressure and running low on money. But it's a whole new thing to be under pressure, low on money, distracted, disappointed, misunderstood, offended, and needing a miracle right away, if not sooner! When several tests hit the believer at the same time, their combined impact is far greater than the force of any of these tests alone.

When The Perfect Storm strikes, it will test the authenticity of your relationship with Christ. And it will reveal what you will do when the winds of controversy, disappointment, confrontation, misunderstanding, delay, distraction, and pressure all seem to collide on your life at the same time.

This test is the grandfather of all tests, and it is Satan's last-ditch effort to keep you from obtaining the blessing that is about to hit your life with a vengeance, if you can only muster up the strength to stay the course and remain faithful to Word of God. There is a man in the Bible who knew a little something about The Perfect Storm.

> And there came a messenger unto Job and said, The oxen were plowing, and the asses were feeding beside them: and the Sabeans fell upon them, and took them away; yea, they have slain the servants with the edge of the sword; and I only am escaped alone to tell thee.
>
> While he was yet speaking, there came also another, and said, The fire of God has fallen from heaven, and hath burned up the sheep, and the servants, and consumed them; and I only am escaped alone to tell thee.
>
> While he was yet speaking, there came also another, and said, The Chaldeans made out three bands, and fell upon the camels, and carried them away, yea, and slain the servants with the edge of the sword; and I only am escaped alone to tell thee.
>
> While he was yet speaking, there came also another, and said, Thy sons and thy daughters were eating and drinking wine in their eldest brother's house: and behold, there came a great wind from the wilderness, and smote the four corners of the house, and it fell upon the young men, and they are dead, and I only am escaped alone to tell thee.
>
> —JOB 1:14–19

It's one thing to get bad news, but it's another thing altogether to get bad news and have somebody else run up while

197

that person is still talking to give more bad news. And then while that person is giving his bad news, somebody else runs up and interrupts him with worse news. But Job's situation only got worse.

Before long his health declined, and Job found himself covered with sore boils from the bottom of his feet to the top of his head. (See Job 2:3–8.) Then Job's wife—who was supposed to be right there with him, supporting him, helping him, encouraging him, and telling him things like, "We can make it through this storm together"—told him, "This is your storm. You ought to curse God and die." (See Job 2:9.)

This guy went through a storm unlike anything any of us have ever experienced. No matter how bad your circumstance might be or how bad my situation may have been at one time or another, we have never gone through anything like what Job endured.

Thank God we can learn from Job's experience and not have to face the same thing ourselves. Job can teach us a lot about what *not* to do. But he can also teach us what *to* do, because by the end of this story, Job gets his head right, his words right, and his attention right. Then God turned his situation around and gave him twice as much as he had before. Job received double for all of his trouble.

THRUST INTO THE STORM

You find out who your friends are when you're in trouble. When the storm hit, Job received a visit from three of his friends—at least he thought they were his friends.

Now, when Job's three friends heard of all this evil that was come upon him, they came every one from his own place; Eliphaz the Temanite, and Bildad the Shuhite, and Zophar the Naamathite: for they had made an appointment together to come to mourn with him and to comfort him. And when they lifted up their eyes afar off, and knew him not, they lifted up their voice and wept; and they rent every one his mantle, and sprinkled dust upon their heads toward heaven. So they sat down with him upon the ground seven days and seven nights, and none spake a word unto him: for they saw that his grief was very great.

—JOB 2:11–13

The visit from his friends caused Job to go into a deep depression. And the Bible says, "After this opened Job his mouth, and cursed his day" (Job 3:1).

Job considered these guys his friends, and when they showed up at his house, he must have been expecting them to encourage him. He must have thought they were going to bring him a word of prophecy from the Lord. Instead they looked at Job from afar off—at first they didn't even recognize him because he was in such bad shape—and then they started crying. They sat down for seven days and seven nights, and didn't have one encouraging word to say to him, leaving Job feeling like he was all alone in the middle of this storm.

So he cursed his birthday: "Let the day perish wherein I was born, and the night in which it was said, There was a man child conceived. Let that day be darkness; let not God regard it from above, neither let the light shine upon it. Let darkness and the shadow of death stain it; let a cloud dwell upon it; let the blackness of the day terrify it. As for that night, let dark-ness seize upon it; let it not be joined unto the days of the year, let it not come into the number of the months" (Job 3:3–6).

Job was in a terrible mental state. He was not asking, "Why didn't I die yesterday?" He asked, "Why didn't I die coming out of my mother's womb?"

> Lo, let that night be solitary, let no joyful voice come therein. Let them curse it that curse the day, who are ready to raise up their mourning. Let the stars of the twilight thereof be dark; let it look for light, but have none; neither let it see the dawning of the day: Because it shut not up the doors of my mother's womb, nor hid sorrow from mine eyes. Why died I not from the womb? why did I not give up the ghost when I came out of the belly?
>
> —Job 3:7–11

Think about what kind of man this is. This is a man the Bible described as the richest man in Uz. He had more money than anybody in that particular region. Until the perfect storm came, this is a man who'd had a good life. He had a wife and healthy children. He was a successful businessman. He had servants. By all appearances he had everything a person would want. But then a perfect storm hit and affected him so much emotionally and mentally that he regretted the fact that he was ever born.

Job could no longer remember the good old days, nor could he muster up the strength to believe it could ever be good again. That's what happens in The Perfect Storm. The storm hits you from every side at once. Everything around you is so dark that if you don't watch it, the storm will steal your hope and leave you thinking, "I'm going to be in this forever," or, "I would rather not be here at all than have to deal with what I'm dealing with right now."

One thing we can learn from Job is that we need to get past the emotional drama of how we feel in order to hear what God is saying. In the midst of your perfect storm, God is always talking with you. He never leaves you out there by yourself, even when you feel like you're all alone. The Lord was able to turn Job's captive situation into double victory when he stopped being self-focused and prayed for his friends (Job 42:10).

CANDLE IN THE WIND

When the Bible speaks of God giving us direction, it often says He will light our candle. Psalm 18:28, for instance, says, "For thou wilt light my candle: the LORD my God will enlighten my darkness." What is the candle the Word is speaking of? Proverbs 20:27 says, "The spirit of man is the candle of the LORD."

What do you use a candle for? You use a candle when it's dark and you want to see where you're going.

When a storm hits, and it starts getting dark, and your emotions are screaming at you—when the feeling of "I quit" is all over you—you have to muster up enough strength to tell yourself: "I can't listen to my emotions. I have to slow down long enough to listen to what the Lord is saying to me." When God is trying to light your candle and give you direction, He doesn't speak to your emotions. He speaks to your spirit.

This is why it's important that you never make a major

decision when you are sitting in the middle of a tragedy. That's not the time to decide you're going to move to another city. That's not the time to decide to get married or divorced. The voice of your emotions might have some truth in it, but that doesn't mean it's God's voice.

To rise above the storms of life, you must learn to listen to the Spirit of God. You need to pray in the Holy Ghost until you have turned down the volume on your emotions and pumped up the volume on your spirit man. This is how you will hear that still, small voice of the Holy Spirit telling you, "This is what you ought to do right now."

When you start hearing God and obeying the small steps He tells you to make, you'll be pointed in the right direction to get out of the storm. You won't just keep sitting there making things worse by trying to fight against the storm with your emotions.

HEARING AND DOING

Listening for God's voice is the first thing you need to do when you're in the middle of a perfect storm, but then you need to verify that you've done what the Lord instructed. This is vital because there are two reasons you can find yourself in the middle of a perfect storm—because you're *in* the will of God or because you're *out* of it. Jesus explained this in a parable about two men who were both hit by a storm.

> And why call ye me Lord, Lord, and do not the things which I say? Whosoever cometh to me and heareth my sayings, and doeth them, I will shew you to whom he is like: He is a like a man which built an house,

and digged deep, and laid the foundation on a rock: and when the flood arose, the stream beat vehemently upon that house, and could not shake it: for it was founded upon a rock. But he that heareth, and doeth not, is like a man that without a foundation built a house upon the earth; against which the stream did beat vehemently, and immediately it fell; and the ruin of that house was great.

—Luke 6:46–49

We have put ourselves into a lot of perfect storms because we did not listen to the wisdom God was attempting to give us. Sometimes we have to admit we were too pig-headed or so blinded that we didn't do what He said.

Of course God is still merciful enough to see you through it, but you're going to have to at least recognize that you didn't pay attention to the voice of the Holy Spirit. The tendency of human nature is to say, "Well, the Lord knows my heart, and He knows I'm working on that." And that's true. God does know your heart. If you're working on something, God does know you're putting forth an effort. The only problem is, Satan doesn't take a day off to let you catch up.

DANGEROUS TERRITORY

Any time we find ourselves out there in disobedience, we're taking a chance, hoping this is not going be the day when Satan comes poking and prodding, seeking whom he may devour. Since he's not all-knowing, he keeps poking around to see if your hedge is down or if there's a gap in your armor somewhere. If he discovers that the wall is not up as it should be, he'll rush in with that perfect storm.

Satan doesn't play fair. He doesn't bother to gradually increase the severity of his attacks. If he can catch you with your hedge down one time, he's going to try to take you out right then. So we have to be wise enough to say, "I have to live my life in obedience to what I know to do right now."

When you don't know certain things and are ignorant in certain areas, God is willing to extend mercy and grace that will shield you while you're walking in ignorance. But when you know what is right to do and willfully make a wrong decision, you're walking in dangerous territory. You might find yourself in a position where Satan can get an advantage over you and attack before you have an opportunity to get things right.

FLYING IN THE DARK

When we find ourselves in the midst of a perfect storm, the next thing we must do is to refuse to lose faith in the power of God's Word. If there is anyone who knows how to deal with a storm, it's Jesus.

> And the same day, when the even was come, he saith unto them, Let us pass over unto the other side. And when they had sent away the multitude, they took him even as he was in the ship. And there were also with him other little ships. And there arose a great storm of wind, and the waves beat into the ship, so that it was now full. And he was in the hinder part of the ship asleep on a pillow: and they awaken him, and say unto him, Master, carest thou not that we perish? And he arose, and rebuked the wind, and said unto the sea,

Peace, be still. And the wind ceased, and there was a great calm.

—MARK 4:35–39

The attack you find yourself going through is not about you; it's about the Word. Satan's ultimate goal is to see if he can get you to cry uncle and say, "This Word is not working."

At some point this walk of faith boils down to who's going to be the toughest. When you showed up for this fight, were you planning only for a four-round fight? Or did you show up with the mentality that you're going to keep fighting the good fight of faith for as long as it takes? In other words, are you in it to win it?

The enemy is going to lie to you when you are stuck out there in utter darkness, when you can't see your way through, and when you have no idea which direction you're supposed to go. Satan will say, "I thought the Word of God was going to see you through? I thought God supplied your every need? I thought you were walking in healing?"

That's when you must have enough courage to say, "Even if it doesn't look like it, even if it doesn't feel like it, even if nobody else agrees with me, I believe the Word of God. I believe if I've done my part to do what the Word says, then the Word will work for me."

When you're out in the middle of the water, it's hard to get your bearings. North looks like south, and east looks like west. If you're going to make it back to land, you'll have to trust your navigational tools. For born-again believers, our compass is the Word of God. The Bible says, "Seek the LORD while he may be found, call ye upon him while he is near: let the wicked forsake his way, and the unrighteous man his thoughts: and let him return unto the LORD, and he will have mercy upon him; and to our God, for he will abundantly pardon" (Isa. 55:6–7).

We need to stop thinking about how we want to handle the situation and turn to God to see what He says to do. Isaiah 55 goes on to say:

> For my thoughts are not your thoughts, neither are your ways my ways, saith the LORD. For as the heavens are higher than the earth, so are my ways higher than your ways, and my thoughts than your thoughts. For as the rain cometh down, and the snow from heaven, and returneth not thither, but watereth the earth, and maketh it bring forth and bud, that it may give seed to the sower, and bread to the eater: So shall my word be that goeth forth out of my mouth: it shall not return unto me void, but it shall accomplish that which I please, and it shall prosper in the thing whereto I sent it.
>
> —ISAIAH 55:8–11

The word *void* here in the Hebrew means *empty*. God is saying, "My Word won't come back empty-handed." So that tells me, if I'm still sitting empty-handed without my healing, provision, joy, or whatever else God says I should have, the Word of God is still working on it because God gave me His promise that His Word is not going to return empty-handed. So if I don't have my hands filled up yet, I don't give up and cry—I just keep on believing the Word!

When you're in the middle of the perfect storm, your mind will tell you, "This stuff is not working." The moment you give in to that thought, your chances of getting out of that storm are over because faith in the Word of God is your only way out of a perfect storm.

NO MORE STINKIN' THINKIN'

Another thing you must do in the midst of a perfect storm is to give yourself a checkup from the neck up. In other words, you have to adjust your attitude. Ask yourself, "Am I a victim of stinkin' thinkin'?"

What I call stinkin' thinkin' is when you start feeling sorry for yourself and saying, "Nobody cares about me. Everybody's against me. God doesn't even care or else He wouldn't have let this happen!" Paul was a victim of bad thinking and successfully adjusted his attitude when he heard from the Lord.

> And lest I should be exalted above measure through the abundance of the revelations, there was given to me a thorn in the flesh, the messenger of Satan to buffet me, lest I should be exalted above measure. For this thing I besought the Lord thrice, that it might depart from me. And he said unto me, My grace is sufficient for thee: for my strength is made perfect in weakness. Most gladly therefore will I rather glory in my infirmities, that the power of Christ may rest upon me. Therefore I take pleasure in infirmities, in reproaches, in necessities, in persecutions, in distresses for Christ's sake: for when I am weak, then am I strong.
> —2 CORINTHIANS 12:7–10

God did not tell Paul, "Just handle it, and you'll be OK." Actually God was saying, "I've given you enough revelation about the authority of the believer for you to know how to handle this situation. You don't have to come whimpering and crying to Me to bail you out. Just do what I've taught you to do, and you'll win."

That means you have to get rid of that stinkin' thinkin.' Get out of the "pity me" and "woe is me" mode. Start declaring what God said. As long as you are moping around and looking for somebody to pat you on the back and tell you that everything is going to be all right, you will stay stuck out there in the middle of the storm.

You have to adjust your attitude as Paul did. He said, "Most gladly therefore will I rather glory in my infirmities, that the power of Christ may rest upon me." What was he saying? "You're right, God. I know I've got on the inside of me what it takes to deal with this."

There is no sermon like the one inside your heart. You believe the sermon that's inside you more than you believe what anybody else is saying. There may be times when you have to look at yourself eyeball to eyeball in the mirror and say, "I know it's going to be all right. In fact, it's going to be better than all right. I'm coming up, and I'm coming out. I'm not going to stay stuck in the middle of this situation. I'm not going to give in to this. I have won in the name of Jesus. Victory is mine!"

If you wake up the next morning and you don't feel right again, then make it into a series. Preach part two to yourself! If you awake the day after that and you still don't feel good, keep on preaching until you come out!

HELP, PLEASE!

The next key to passing the test of the perfect storm is to refuse to be a loner. Ecclesiastes 4:9–12 says: "Two are better than one; because they have a good reward for their labour. For if they fall, the one will lift up his fellow: but woe to him that is alone when he falleth; for he hath not another to help him up. Again, if two lie together, then they have heat: but how can one be warm alone? And if one prevail against him, two shall withstand him; and a threefold cord is not quickly broken."

One of Satan's chief tactics is to convince you that nobody cares and everybody is against you—that you are alone in your struggles. But you can't be a loner in the middle of a storm. You need other people. You have to recognize that God has put people in your life to help you. Most importantly, in the middle of a perfect storm, when you need help, you have to be willing to receive it.

In the movie *The Perfect Storm* the little fishing boat tragically encountered a giant wave. When the crew recovered the *Andrea Gail,* they found that her emergency distress radio beacon—which would have enabled the Coast Guard to find them—had been accidentally turned off.[1] Of course everyone who knew the men on the *Andrea Gail* were out in the storm wanted to see them rescued, but nobody could find them. Without even realizing it, these distressed fishermen weren't sending out a signal that said, "Come and find me."

So often, when you're in the middle of a perfect storm, you can inadvertently give off signals that you don't want or need anybody's help by disappearing and not returning people's calls. As the crew of the *Andrea Gail* learned, it's just as incumbent upon the one who's in trouble to send out a distress signal as it is for the rescue team to respond to that cry for help and come rushing to their aid.

In order to allow other people to help you, your heart must be open and say, "C'mon and help me!" Of course, you can't dictate how the help comes or who it comes from (because sometimes God will send you help from some of the most unlikely sources).

I think a lot of people end up stuck in a perfect storm because their pride doesn't want anybody to know what they're going through. But it's foolish to let your whole marriage go down the drain because you don't want to receive counseling. Our ultimate goal as Christians ought to be to win. I want to win in my marriage. I want to win with my family. I want to win with my children. I just want to win!

SOMEBODY'S WATCHING YOU

In the Book of Acts, Paul encounters a storm that the King James Bible calls a "Euroclydon" (Acts 27:14). In the Amplified Bible, this same storm is called a "northeaster"—which is the exact type of storm the *Andrea Gail* faced in October 1991, the one that meteorologists called a "perfect storm."

Since Paul actually experienced and survived a perfect storm, if anybody can give us some advice and direction on how to get out of one, it ought to be him. The apostle Paul had warned those with him in the boat that he perceived the trip was going to be dangerous, but the head centurion wouldn't listen.

But not long after there arose against it a tempestuous wind, called Euroclydon. And when the ship was caught, and could not bear up into the wind, we let her drive. And running under a certain island which is called Clauda, we had much work to come by the boat: Which when they had taken up, they used helps, undergirding the ship; and, fearing lest they should fall into the quicksands, strake sail, and so were driven. And we being exceedingly tossed with a tempest, the next day they lightened the ship; and the third day we cast out with our own hands the tackling of the ship. And when neither sun nor stars in many days appeared, and no small tempest lay on us, all hope that we should be saved was then taken away.

—Acts 27:14–20

So what do you do when all natural hope is gone?

But after long abstinence Paul stood forth in the midst of them, and said, Sirs, ye should have hearkened unto me, and not have loosed from Crete, and to have gained this harm and loss. And now I exhort you to be of good cheer: for there shall be no loss of any man's life among you, but of the ship. For there stood by me this night the angel of God, whose I am, and whom I serve.

—Acts 27:21–23

When all natural hope is gone, you need to remind yourself to whom you belong. When there's no reason at all for you to believe your situation can be turned around, you need to remember that you're not out there by yourself. When there's no reason for you to lift your head up and believe things can be better than they are at that moment, you need to remind yourself: "I am still on the Lord's side, and the Lord is still on my side."

> For there stood by me this night the angel of God, whose I am, and whom I serve, Saying, Fear not, Paul; thou must be brought before Caesar: and, lo, God hath given thee all them that sail with thee.
>
> And while the day was coming on, Paul besought them all to take meat, saying, This day is the four-teenth day that ye have tarried and continued fasting, having taken nothing. Wherefore I pray you to take some meat: for this is for your health: for there shall not an hair fall from the head of any of you. And when he had thus spoken, he took bread, and gave thanks to God in presence of them all: and when he had broken it, he began to eat. Then were they all of good cheer, and they also took some meat. And we were in all in the ship two hundred threescore and sixteen souls.
>
> —ACTS 27:23–24, 33–37

When you're going through the perfect storm, you're also winning the battle for others. You'll notice that Paul didn't say, "Oh, well, it's not working out. But I'm born again, so Master, here I come to join you in heaven." There were 275 other people on that ship. Paul knew he had to get the victory over this perfect storm not only for himself but also for the people whose lives were dependent on him.

No matter what level you're on, someone is always watching you. One day when that person finds himself in the midst of trouble, he can come and ask you, "What did you do to get through your tough time?"

As the story about Paul continues, you find out that everyone made it out of the storm safely because Paul had enough good sense to seek God for a word. Once on land some people might have let down their guard. However, Paul knew there is no resting and relaxing for a soldier in the Lord's army. Almost immediately he was faced with a new crisis.

> And when they were escaped, then they knew that the island was called Melita. And the barbarous people shewed us no little kindness: for they kindled a fire, and received us every one, because of the present rain, and because of the cold. And when Paul had gathered a bundle of sticks, and laid them on the fire, there came a viper out of the heat, and fastened on his hand. And when the barbarians saw the venomous beast hang on his hand, they said among themselves, No doubt this man is a murderer, whom, though he hath escaped the sea, yet vengeance suffereth not to live. And he shook off the beast into the fire, and felt no harm.
>
> —ACTS 28:1–5

You have to make up your mind. Either you are a soldier in the army of the Lord, or you are not. If you are, then you need to be prepared for whatever test comes next. You need to say, "Not only am I getting through this perfect storm, but when I get through this, I'll also be ready for whatever else may come my way." You can't let yourself get so focused on the storm you're going through now that you forget you may not get a break before some new problem arises.

After the snake bit him, I believe Paul had an attitude that said, "I have done everything I needed to do to survive this storm. There is no way I'm going to get taken out by some snake coming out of the fire." But it was just a little attitude. The Bible doesn't say, "He swung the viper and smashed it on the ground." It says he shook it off.

I believe Paul had an attitude that told the problem, "You have the nerve, after what I've already been through? You have the audacity to think something as small as you is going to take me out when I just came through a perfect storm?" Then he shook the snake off.

HERE COMES THE SUN

You may find yourself thrust into a perfect storm right now. It might be raining cats and dogs in your life. It may look like all hell is breaking loose. It might seem like everything that could go wrong has started to go wrong. But I'm here to tell you, that storm is passing over!

If you're going through a perfect storm, you need to give the Lord some praise in advance. Praise Him like the storm is over and thank Him that you're coming out. It may be a perfect storm, but you serve a perfect God, and your perfect God will defeat the perfect storm every single time!

There is a big difference between the perfect storm the crew of the *Andrea Gail* experienced and the perfect storm you may be going through. The difference is that you are not the captain of your own ship. You have someone at the helm who has been there and done that. He's leading your vessel. He's the One guiding you through the storms. He's the One who's driving your ship to safety.

If you'll just hang on and keep doing what the Holy Spirit is telling you to do and never stop trusting Him, before long you'll see the sun starting to break through the dark clouds. When you make it to the other side of this perfect storm, you'll find that the sun has been shining the entire time, and all along God has been trying to get you over to this bright, sunshiny day.

DISCUSSION QUESTIONS

1. Discuss a time when you or someone you know went through a perfect storm. What important lessons did you learn from the experience?

2. What do you believe is Satan's ultimate goal in bringing a perfect storm your way? Why?

3. What preparations do you need to make today to ensure you are ready to face The Perfect Storm?

Conclusion

L ET'S JUST SETTLE one thing right now: Most of the tests we've looked at in this book are just not fair. You're minding your own business, then stuff from your past comes knocking on the door. That's not fair!

You didn't do anything wrong, but someone misunderstands your actions or motives. That's not fair!

You are unfairly attacked or insulted, and yet you're expected to not feel hurt. That's not fair! You're sailing on smooth seas under clear skies one minute, and the next you're being tossed around by a perfect storm. That's not fair!

But whoever said life would be fair?

If you desire to grow as a believer and advance to higher levels of responsibility and accountability in the kingdom of God, then you will have to learn to deal with unfair and unexpected situations. That is the only way you can pass the tests of life. Leadership is laced with unfair circumstances. No one ever said everything would be fair about helping other people reach a place that would benefit them.

Your promotion to higher levels of leadership in the kingdom of God depends upon your ability to handle whatever comes against you in a way that pleases God. Those who sit around and cry about how unfair things are will never make it.

I wrote this book to help you understand why you are going through difficult times and why some of the challenges you are facing have come your way. As you pass each test, you will progress to the next level of spiritual maturity.

I want to encourage you to pay attention to all the tests we looked at together. Keep this book handy so you can remind yourself of what you've learned. Remember, if you ever find yourself wondering why some bad thing has happened to you or someone you love, there's probably a test involved.

Always keep in mind that whenever one of these tests comes your way, you should do what you can to pass it right away. That's because if you don't pass the test the first time around, you'll have to take it again (and again and again and again) until you do pass it.

After you pass a test in one area of your life, you may face a similar test in a different area. So it's important that you always stay alert. For example, you may pass The Test of Being Misunderstood among members of your family. But then six months later you discover you've been misunderstood at work—and you have to pass that test again.

If you fail a test, you will stay stuck in the same spot. God is not going to promote you if you can't handle a situation the way the Word tells you to handle it. So when something comes up in your life, remind yourself that there's probably a reason you have to deal with it. And instead of complaining about how bad you feel or how unhappy you are, just learn the lesson and pass the test so you don't have to retake it.

Finally, my friend, if you've just realized that you're going through one of these tests right now, don't get depressed or discouraged about it. In fact, you ought to get excited! The only reason you're taking this test at this time is because you're one step away from promotion. And that's great news, because right now you know everything you need to know to pass *every* test with flying colors! Declare this with me:

> *In the name of Jesus, I declare that I will pass all the tests of life. I will pass every single test, every single time, from this day forward.*
>
> *I make up my mind and purpose in my heart that I will watch for these tests and not be deceived or confused. I will recognize when I'm taking a test, and I will do what I have learned in order to pass. And if I miss it and fail a test, I purpose in my heart to quickly get it right.*
>
> *I know God has an awesome destiny for me. I know I'm going somewhere to do something great for the kingdom of God. In the name of Jesus, I'm passing the tests of life, I'm walking in victory, and I'm experiencing promotion and increase. I declare that the best is yet to come for me and my house, in Jesus's name. Amen.*

Notes

CHAPTER FOUR
THE DISTRACTION TEST

1. *Noah Webster's 1828 American Dictionary*, s.v. "distract," http://
www.1828-dictionary.com/d/word/distract (accessed February 8, 2012).

CHAPTER SIX
THE TEST OF BEING MISUNDERSTOOD

1. Dictionary.com, *Collins English Dictionary Complete &*
Unabridged 10th Edition (n.p.: William Collins Sons & Co. Ltd./Harper-
Collins Publishers, 2009), s.v. "misunderstood," http://dictionary
.reference.com/browse/misunderstood (accessed February 8, 2012).

CHAPTER TEN
THE OFFENSE TEST

1. *Merriam-Webster*, s.v. "offense", http://www.merriam-webster.com/
dictionary/offense?show=0&t=1328547293 (accessed February 6, 2012).

2. Freedictoinary.com, s.v. "fretful," http://www.thefreedictionary
.com/fretful (accessed February 6, 2012).

3. *Merriam-Webster*, s.v. "resent," http://www.merriam-webster.com/
dictionary/resent (accessed February 6, 2012).

CHAPTER TWELVE
THE PERFECT STORM

1. National Climatic Data Center, National Oceanic and Atmospheric
Administration, "The Perfect Storm: October 1991," http://www.ncdc
.noaa.gov/oa/satellite/satelliteseye/cyclones/pfctstorm91/pfctstorm.html
(accessed February 8, 2012).

About the Author

BISHOP GEORGE L. Davis and his wife, April, are the senior pastors of Faith Christian Center in Jacksonville, Florida. Faith Christian Center was founded in 1996 with twelve members and has since grown into a thriving congregation of more than four thousand. Bishop Davis also oversees churches in Orlando, Florida; Tampa, Florida; Miami, Florida; Tallahassee, Florida; Valdosta, Georgia; Hampton, Georgia; Norfolk, Virginia; and Piura, Peru.

In addition to planting churches and mentoring pastors, Bishop Davis is the host of a weekly television broadcast, *Born to Win*; the publisher of a bimonthly magazine, *Family Life Now*; and a much sought-after church and conference speaker. Through the international missions and outreach programs of George Davis Ministries, he is taking the life-changing message of victory through Christ into South Korea, Uganda, Haiti, the Dominican Republic, Bulgaria, and many other nations of the world.

Bishop Davis graduated from the Word of Faith School of Ministry in Detroit, Michigan, and graduated summa cum laude from the University of North Florida with a bachelor's degree in business. He and his wife are the parents of three beautiful children.